Hoarder Homes:

Piles of Hazards for Firefighters

RYAN PENNINGTON

Ryan Pennington

Jumpscat Training LLC

2015

Copyright © 2015

Ryan Pennington

All rights reserved. This book or any portion thereof may not be reproduced or used in any manner whatsoever without the express written permission of the publisher except for the use of brief quotations in a book review or scholarly journal.

Editing: Laura Sumner (lauramsumner@yahoo.com)

First Printing: 2015

ISBN-13: 978-1515375821

ISBN-10: 151537582X

Jumpseat Training LLC

Charleston, WV 25313

Ryan Pennington

The content of this book is provided for informational purposes only. Firefighting is an inherently deadly activity where thousands of firefighters are injured and hundreds die yearly. Always use extreme caution when carrying out any fire department related activity and follow all safety guidelines set forth.

The information and content found in this book are intended for firefighters who are certified by their respective local authority. The use of this information is done at your own risk and no fault or liability is placed upon Jumpseat Training LLC.

DEDICATION

This book is dedicated to the men and women of the fire service. Over the past 20+ years so many people have helped me along the way and having served with, met, and experienced the sacrifices that come with a life of service, this book is my way of paying it forward.

To my loving wife Heather, you are my world. 16 years ago God placed you in my life for a purpose. Your love, support, understanding, and sacrifice means more than you will ever know. Your unwavering support is an amazing gift.

To my son David Dylan, I am so proud of you. Watching you grow into a man has been a huge honor. From a young boy, to a collegiate basketball player, and now on to a solider in the Army National Guard, your journey has just begun. I cannot wait to see you progress in the next years into a soldier, husband, teacher, and Commissioned Officer. Go out and seek out challenges while remembering your mother and I support you 100%!

My dear daughter Alyson, you are the light of my life. You are a true gift from God. I have never met another young lady with your humor, compassion, understanding, talent, and vocabulary. The world is yours Alyson; it's up to you to seize the moments. You have begun the journey into womanhood with grace, poise, and style.

I love our chats, texts, and talks about horses. (All the while you know I don't like horses.) I so look forward to watching you follow in Dylan's footsteps into college and beyond. I will hold you to your promise of graduating college, becoming the first from my side of the Penningtons to do so. Keep your smile and chase your dreams!

To all firefighters from around the world! My challenge to you is to keep pushing the limits of understanding. The research in the pages of this book was long, hard, and took me on a journey to understand different opinions.

If we don't allow new ideas to surface we will stay stagnant and not progress our profession. Don't take this information as any more than ideas to take back to your departments and test. Some ideas will work and some might not. It's up to you to find out what applies and what doesn't.

Seek out these solutions, set up drills, conduct burns, and validate them in the context of your department.

When you do, shoot me an email JumpseatViews@Icloud.com.

I want to hear them.

To Peter Matthews, my friend - I could NEVER repay you for the opportunities you have given me over the past six years. Your friendship, guidance, and strong direction mean the world to this jumpseat rider. Thank you for all the support!

Finally, to my mentor Dr. Rich Gasaway. When I decided to write this book I had only one person in mind to write the forward. To say you have changed my life would be a massive understatement. Guiding me from a being a car salesman to a three-time published author, firefighter, instructor, podcaster, and keynote speaker, your mark on my life is obvious.

When you finally decide to retire and enjoy life, know this my friend. Your influence on the fire service will continue as I carry it with me everywhere I teach - paying you back by paying it forward.

Ryan

CONTENTS

Dedication 7

Acknowledgements 13

Foreword 15

Chapter 1: 21

Chapter 2: 29

Chapter 3: 43

Chapter 4: 71

Chapter 5: 81

Chapter 6: 97

Chapter 7: 103

Chapter 8: 119

Chapter 9: 133

Chapter 10: 143

Chapter 11: 179

Chapter 12: 199

Chapter 13: 217

Chapter 14: 225

Chapter 15: 235

Notes 245

Sample Heavy Content SOG 248

References 253

About the Author 257

ACKNOWLEDGEMENTS

Without the support and help of some key people this book and the corresponding research would not have been possible. Thanking them would take months but I would like to take the time to thank a few key folks for their help. Joe Starnes, you challenged me to think outside the box and offered the opportunity to conduct live fire research at Kill the Flashover 2015. I will be forever grateful.

To my Band of Brothers, you guys are my rock and you friendship means the world to me. Mike Daley, John Dixon, John Hayowyk, Rob Fling, Andy Starnes, Dan Kerrigan, Rob Owens, Scotty Symonds, Jim Moss, and Chris Baker you guys ROCK!

Lastly to my WV fire friends. Dave Wagoner, Corey Carr, and Richie Gobble III thank you for your hard work and being the go-to firefighters during the KTF burns. Having you three on the line was amazing and reassuring that the line was ready for battle.

To the #JumpseatNation, thank each and every one of you and make sure you stay #JumpseatReady!

FOREWORD

I have had the privilege of knowing Ryan Pennington for more than 15 years. We first met in 1997 in, of all places, an AOL chat room themed for people with an interest in the fire service. At the time, chat rooms were one of the few places online where firefighters could go to share ideas, air frustrations and learn from fellow firefighters from around the world. I don't recall exactly what we talked about in that first discussion but we hit it off because we had two things in common. We were both from West Virginia and we both loved serving as firefighters.

Back in those days Ryan was serving as a volunteer firefighter and shared with me his aspirations to make it his career. He was working a job that didn't pay very well and he confided in me that he didn't have the discretionary income to pay for EMT class. He had the ambition but he lacked the financial means to kick-start his career. So I told him to enroll in the class and I would pay for it. And he did. It was a leap of faith on my part sending money to someone I had never met. But the gamble paid off.

While we stayed in touch, many years would pass before Ryan and I would ever have the opportunity to meet in person. I was working as a fire chief in Ohio and through our many online chats Ryan knew a lot about my department and the innovative things we were doing, and he wanted to get a first-hand look. He traveled three hours to spend a couple of days riding along with our crews. He asked a lot of good questions, and it affirmed to me that he was truly dedicated to being a firefighter.

As time marched on I was fortunate to coach Ryan in his career development, which including getting his paramedic certification in 2000. The big payoff for all his hard work came in 2007 when he was sworn in to serve as a firefighter-paramedic for the City of Charleston Fire Department. Unfortunately I couldn't attend his ceremony but I was cheering him on from afar.

Time marched on and my career took me on to Minnesota for a new fire chief's job. Ryan and I met up again in 2009 at the Firehouse Expo in Baltimore. There I introduced him to Peter Matthews, the Editor-in-Chief of firehouse.com. As fate would have it, Peter was looking for content contributors and Ryan was looking for a way to share his knowledge. And share he has contributing over 100 articles themed around his Views from the Jumpseat and hoarding topics.

The one thing that has been consistent along the way is Ryan's gratitude for my coaching and support. He often says he doesn't know how he will repay me. To which I have consistently responded. "Pay it forward, Ryan. Simply do for others as I have done for you. Give back. Share your knowledge."

After a fire in a home with hoarded conditions Ryan was inspired to write about his experience. In his research for his article, he quickly realized there wasn't much out there on the topic of hoarding challenges for first responders. So he set out to change that. He knew there were many lessons to learn and much to be shared.

He has worked passionately to develop programs and to launch a website to share his experiences and the experiences of others challenged with providing emergency services in hoarded environments. He launched the Chamber of Hoarders website and started blogging. Since then, he has presented on the topic of hoarding to thousands of first responders throughout the United States and Canada. Turns out, hoarding is a BIG DEAL and there are many first responders suffering injuries and deaths while trying to mitigate emergencies in these homes.

One of the challenges firefighters were facing was what to call a hoarded environment, especially in the presence of the owner of all that "stuff." I recommended to Ryan that he come up with a special term that described the contents without being offensive to the owner of all that contents. As a result of some brainstorming over the phone one evening the term "Heavy Contents" was born. Heavy describes both the quantity and weight of the contents and avoids the use of terms that can upset a customer.

Ryan then took the term and developed more program content, shared more on his blog, developed a DVD and online academy, and now offers you this book – the first definitive guide to hoarding dangers for first responders.

This book provides a fascinating and sometimes disturbing look into the history of compulsive hoarding and how the fire service has been forced to deal with this growing addiction to accumulate contents. The book offers tangible solutions to this unique safety issue, including introducing you to a clutter rating scale, sharing how to make a size-up, search for occupants, attack the fire, manage your air supply, conduct rapid intervention, perform overhaul and more. He even addresses hoarding for EMS and fire prevention personnel.

I am honored that Ryan asked me to make a small contribution to this book. As you read it, keep an open mind and know that what he's sharing with you has been well-researched and practiced in many evolutions. I will close by noting this book fits in very well with my situational awareness mission helping you see the bad things coming... in time to avoid bad outcomes. Thanks for paying it forward, Ryan.

Dr. Richard B. Gasaway, EFO, CFO
Fire chief (ret.)
Founder and Editor
Situational Awareness Matters! Preface

CHAPTER 1:
WHAT YOU DON'T KNOW MAY KILL YOU

Responding to emergencies inside conditions caused by Compulsive Hoarding Disorder poses an increased risk to the responders when compared to a non-cluttered environment. Dangers found inside these cluttered environments included biohazard exposure, increased risk of rapid fire phenomenon, and constant risk of structural collapse. It is important for responders to understand these dangers and learn ways to reduce the risk presented by each.

My research over the past three years confirms that the challenges faced by first responders when dealing with cluttered conditions have been increasing. From near miss incidents to line of duty deaths, the dangers have been evident.

One example was seen in Shoreview, Minnesota. The Shoreview case was a structure fire with a confirmed occupant that burned for an estimated eight to ten hours before discovery. Once the fire department arrived and discovered the interior cluttered conditions, their efforts were severely slowed. Luckily the slowed operations allowed firefighters to discover that the flooring had been burned through, causing a direct hole into a cluttered basement (Horner, S., 2012).

In the case of Shoreview, the clutter actually saved the firefighters from potentially falling into the basement. Had it not been for the clutter they would have used normal search strategies while looking for the occupant. Normal primary searches are performed swiftly in a systematic approach that keeps the firefighters oriented to a wall. This method would have reduced the time taken to discover burned-through flooring. The fire department, in this case the Lake Johanna Fire Department, described an extremely cluttered interior and expressed concern for the extended burn time suspected in this case (Personal Communication, 2013).

The inspiration to research hoarding came from my home department's experience during a rescue attempt of an occupant from cluttered conditions on Kanawha Avenue in Charleston, West Virginia. During the attempted rescue of the occupant, four firefighters were injured and transported to a local hospital. The injuries were caused by smoke inhalation, exhaustion, and a fall through the floor into the basement. All of the firefighters treated that evening received only minor injuries. They were fortunate that one, if not all, of the injuries did not escalate into a line of duty death. During the after action review of this particular rescue, I began to see the need for adjustments while operating in cluttered conditions.

Being a typical Generation X person, the first place I turned to was Google. What I found (or didn't find) was simply amazing. Very few articles, and only one study, on hoarding-related fires were the only things that turned up. Most of the articles were very generic and only offered a glimpse into what a hoarding disorder is or hoarding's history as related to the fire service. Not one article or study introduced the reader to the cues and clues that would indicate hoarding inside a building or suggested any tactical changes when dealing with a cluttered environment.

This lack of available information is what led me to begin the research process into firefighting in a cluttered environment. During the early stages I found astonishing similarities in the challenges and outcomes as each fire department described its responses to this type of fire. Using these case studies, some independent learning, and fire research, I developed solutions to address this growing issue.

Deciding on this education model led to writing articles and developing a class, and drove my passion to become an authority on this topic. The constant writing and teaching has affectionately gained me a new nickname, Ryan the "hoarder guy".

Many fire departments have introduced the necessary changes and thought processes after attending the class. The Shawnee, Kansas, Fire Department's Deputy Fire Chief Sal Scarpa wrote, "Ryan's presentation was engaging and timely. He offered many practical observations that we were able to put to use it immediately for our department. Moreover, his presentation opened up a dialogue between our department and our Police Department concerning this problem. The result has been a reciprocal agreement to provide each other with intelligence on hoarder homes. Thank you, Ryan for bringing your energy and passion to the Kansas City region. You have certainly made an impact for the Shawnee Fire Department," (Scarpa, S., 2014).

Another example of a success story followed shortly

after a full day presentation at the Creekside Volunteer Fire Department. A firefighter that attended that presentation sent an anonymous message describing a hoarding fire. The firefighter wrote, "We were making an aggressive interior attack when I began to notice the clutter was increasing in height and density. I immediately went back to your discussion during the class at the Creekside Volunteer Fire Department.

Your words that told us to pay close attention if the clutter was beginning to increase in height and the dangers provided by that height played through my mind. Taking this all into consideration, myself and the other firefighter made the determination to back out of the house and go defensive. Later in the operation we discovered that if we would have continued to crawl on the path that we were taking, we would have fallen into the basement through a hole that was created from burned floor joists underneath the weight of a piano. There is no doubt that your words saved not only my life, but the life of the firefighter that was with me," (Anonymous, 2014).

These two examples are the fuel that fires my passion for protecting both citizens and responders from these dangers. Sharing what I have learned about hoarding has quickly become my life's purpose. Adding fuel to this burning passion is the fact that I have a family member who suffers from Compulsive Hoarding Disorder that I am unable to help. Her compulsion to collect and store massive amounts of belongings overrides my care, compassion, and desire to protect her from the dangers of hoarding.

Being exposed to the family's side of this issue has allowed me to share the need for compassion and caring when dealing with the afflicted occupant. Having the perspectives of both the family and the first responder also allows for a comprehensive view on how deep-seated an issue this really is.

Now, my offer to you as we progress through this book is this: I will share the stories, research, and solutions that I have discovered in a systematic approach to dealing with these issues. It is up to you how open your mind is to new thought processes and tactics and how you can apply them to your District and responses. I am not here to sell you on some new whiz bang tool or some revolutionary way of fighting fires. As a matter of fact, we will be spending a lot of the time on tried and true methods of fire attack, and even some throwback tools and procedures that many fire departments have not used in years. A Bresnan distributor nozzle and piercing nozzles are two examples of such tools.

If you take the time to read this material, understand the concepts, and practice the tactics, you will add an extra layer of safety when, not if, you respond to a cluttered environment.

Moving forward into the next chapter, it is important to understand what Compulsive Hoarding Disorder is, who can be affected by the disorder, common characteristics of a cluttered environment, and some of the challenges faced when dealing with the afflicted occupant.

In the fire service, customer service should be the top priority on all responses. Just because you're dealing with an occupant that is afflicted with Compulsive Hoarding Disorder does not give you the right to treat them any differently.

Let's begin our journey by learning about the disorder.

CHAPTER 2:
INTRODUCTION TO COMPULSIVE HOARDING DISORDER

Compulsive Hoarding Disorder is defined as the accumulation of and failure to discard a large number of objects that seem to have little to no apparent value. This collection grows until the rooms are not usable for their intended purposes. It is believed that somewhere between five to seven percent of people are affected by this disorder, with the true number of afflicted unknown and likely to grow (Bratiotis, Schmalish & Steketee, 2011). Some popular television shows have revealed the hidden struggles of those dealing with massive amounts of belongings.

In 2013, hoarding was added to the newest edition of the Diagnostic and Statistical Manual of Mental Disorders (DSM), the "bible" for mental health professionals (American Psychiatric Association,

2013). Up until this point, hoarding had been considered a form of Obsessive Compulsive Disorder (OCD), and studies have shown that people who hoard can have OCD-like symptoms. However, they are not consistent with every case of hoarding.

Now that Compulsive Hoarding Disorder has been added to the DSM-V, it can be isolated and studied for causation and treatment separate from OCD. Compulsive Hoarding has only been studied for approximately 15 years. This may sound like a long time, but when compared to the length of time we have studied cancer or heart disease, we are still early in the process of studying this complex disorder.

Being in the early stages of research, many things have yet to be fully understood. Why do people hoard? What causes them to attach deep emotional feelings to things that have no apparent value? What are some factors that increase these feelings? These are just a few of the variables being studied by the mental health community. Some answers are coming out and some questions will have no answers in the near future.

Compulsive Hoarding Disorder has been documented in all countries, age ranges, races, and covers all income levels. It crosses all borders and can be found in any neighborhood. This finding dispels many of the pre-conceived notions that this disorder only affects the poor or elderly. Hoarding has been diagnosed in people as young as 13. Knowing that this disorder can be found in all areas of the world, first responders should be trained to deal with the dangers caused by hoarding.

(Figure 2-1: The Collection has begun in this bedroom making access harder if the bedroom was to be searched. Photo Credit Author)

People who suffer from compulsive hoarding disorder assign great value to items that have no apparent value. It is common for them to assign the same value to a stack of newspapers that a non-affected person would assign to their children's baby pictures or wedding photos. Receiving these positive feelings compels them to accumulate belongings from various locations and by using different means of acquisition. As their belongings accumulate, so does the positive feeling from collecting this great volume of "treasures." This perceived great "value" is where first responders can run into challenges when dealing with a hoarding fire (Figure 2-1).

Just as the affected person receives positive feelings from accumulating belongings, he receives negative feelings when faced with parting ways with them. Throwing away the perceived "treasures" causes great anguish and stress. Such deep emotional attachment to these belongings can lead to a stress level that has been documented to cause a heart attack in an afflicted person (Frost, Steketee, 2010). The inability to part ways with these belongings can lead an afflicted person to fill any available space. Dr. Randy Frost describes this as "filling any container available." (R. Frost, Personal Communication, 2014).

As a result of the affected person's inability to part with his belongings, a compulsive hoarder will begin to fill his surroundings with a variety of things. The collection can start to take over his home and make rooms unusable for their intended purpose (Figure 2-

2). Filling the home until he is unable to function exposes the occupant to many dangers from fires, falls, collapse, and other biological hazards. It's these hazards that often stay hidden until the occupant has an emergency and calls for help, making the emergency responders the first people to discover the conditions.

(Figure 2-2: The occupant is unable to use this room due to their collection. Dix Hills Long Island Fire Dept came across this condition on an assist call. Photo Credit Rob Fling)

Many people afflicted by Compulsive Hoarding Disorder stay "hidden" from their surroundings. They tend to be very reclusive, introverted, and keep to themselves, while taking great lengths to hide the condition of the home's interior. Their feelings of embarrassment, shame, and guilt will keep family members, neighbors, and other visitors out of the home as the occupant will not want to be "found out" or discovered. It is common for people who are afflicted with this disorder to understand their condition and feel embarrassed and ashamed. Having these feelings often compels them to stay inside their homes and not interact with the outside world.

There are documented cases where hoarders have placed booby-traps to protect their perceived valuable collections (Frost, Steketee, 2010). They make traps to hurt anyone that tries to access, steal, or grab parts of their treasures. While this sounds extreme, it illustrates how compelled some hoarders are to protect their collections. This compulsion can cause major problems for first responders that try to move or remove these treasures in an emergency situation. Compulsive hoarding creates a space that is no longer usable for its intended purpose, thereby making it difficult to walk through, much less conduct a search or attack a fire. The mountains of debris will limit the ability to maneuver through a home to a trapped occupant or to the seat of the fire.

One thing that is consistent in every case of hoarding is the inability to organize belongings as they are accumulated (Frost, Steketee, 2010). The piles begin to get higher as hoarders fail to throw items away. It's the contents of these piles that add an unknown danger to first responders (similar to highly piled storage in a warehouse). These stacks may be comprised of any number of things. Each accumulation has its own set of risks. Therefore, firefighters must adjust for the stacks and move away from conventional methods of response.

Hoarders can collect many different items, including those that pose unreasonable risks to firefighters, such as large volumes of newspapers, magazines, plastics of different types, and other belongings that can fuel a fire. In the Collyer brothers' case, which we will review shortly, an estimated 20,000 books were removed from the house (Frost, Steketee, 2010).

There are often many false assumptions associated with individuals afflicted with Compulsive Hoarding Disorder:

- Hoarders are selfish
- Hoarders are lazy
- It only affects the poor
- More women are affected than men

- Hoarding is a choice
- It only affects the uneducated

(Bratiotis, et al., 2011)

These beliefs could not be further from the truth. Research has shown that many people afflicted with Compulsive Hoarding Disorder have a very giving and thoughtful nature. They purchase something with the intent of giving it to someone. Purchasing the item gives positive feelings knowing that they will be giving a gift soon. However, with Compulsive Hoarding Disorder, the negative feelings start when an item is lost or given away. While the intent is to give them away, parting with it comes with negative feelings, and so the item remains with the afflicted person (Frost, Steketee, 2010).

This problem is common when dealing with compulsive hoarders. This cycle will continue again and again until the piles of belongings take over one's home.

Another misconception of compulsive hoarding is that it affects more women than men. It has been shown that Compulsive Hoarding Disorder affects more men than women, but women seek help more often for their disorder (Bratiotis, et al., 2011). This clouds the statistics, as the true number of men afflicted is as yet undetermined.

People who have Compulsive Hoarding Disorder are often aware of their disorder and feel ashamed, embarrassed, or afraid of being "found out" as the ramifications of this could be a forced "clean out" or their secret being "let out." Many times they will not even allow their family members to enter their homes, adding to the mystery of how much and what they are accumulating.

That hoarders are "uneducated" and "poor" are huge misconceptions associated with Compulsive Hoarding Disorder. The compulsion to collect does cross all economic levels and has been proven to affect many well-educated individuals. In fact, many educated, "eccentric" people are affected by the disorder. From nuclear physicists to college professors, it appears to be more prevalent with those who are more highly educated.

"Hoarding is a choice!" Now that Compulsive Hoarding Disorder has its own, specific diagnosis, much more has been discovered, including that it is *not* a choice. Compulsive hoarding is a mental disorder. Many times people begin to accumulate belongings as a choice, but the disorder occurs when they begin to hang onto the collection and discover they cannot part with any of it. Some common factors have been identified as triggers leading to a person starting to hoard. Stressful life events such as divorce, bankruptcy, the death of a friend or family member, or loss of a job can lead to the beginnings of the hoarding affliction (Bratiotis, et al., 2011). In the deepness of his pain, a person starts to receive positive feelings from collecting belongings. Often, these are the belongings of the person that has caused the feelings, such as the loved one who has died or the spouse who left him.

Collecting these worldly possessions helps to ease the pain and suffering that they are feeling. As a coping mechanism, the compulsion to collect begins, and continues until he cannot stand the thought of parting with his belongings. Experiencing a stressful life event has been a common factor in many people affected with hoarding disorder and is believed to be a major cause.

Another contributing factor is the environment in which a person was raised. Being raised in a hoarding environment may lead to the children of the hoarder being affected with the same disorder. If someone is raised in this type of environment and exposed to the mindset of the hoarder as a child, they can often take on this behavior later in life. Believing such an environment to be "normal" can compel the children of hoarders to start the collection of belongings in their own homes as they age (Children of Hoarding, 2015). Many people learn their values from their parents, so to have this issue passed along from parents to children makes sense.

Inside the Collyers' Mansion

One of the first known reports of hoarders happened in Manhattan, New York. Homer and Langley Collyer were brothers who lived in a brownstone apartment. Both brothers were college educated, "eccentric" individuals who lived together their entire lives. Their brownstone was located on the corner of 128th Street and was packed to capacity with books, furniture, musical instruments, and many other items, including booby-traps set to catch anyone who would try to steal from them.

The Collyer brothers' hoard was quite fascinating, as they collected everything from books to grand pianos. This case of hoarding was a great example of how a building can fall into disrepair when the weight of the contents begins to affect the structural integrity of the building. Both Collyer brothers died inside their brownstone as Homer's health faded and Langley took care of him.

The neighbors became worried about the two brothers and the police were notified. Once they pushed their way through an upstairs window they found Homer Collyer passed away and Langley nowhere to be found. A missing person report was issued for him as the cleanup began. The authorities removed 136 tons of material during the cleanup, including the body of Langley himself.

It appeared that Langley had fallen victim to one of his booby-traps while taking Homer food and may have perished before Homer. The building had to be torn down during the cleanup process and today you can find a memorial there for the brothers. Since their passing, the Fire Department of New York has called cluttered homes "Collyers' Mansions" (Frost, Steketee, 2010).

Many common traits recognized in hoarder homes today were found in the Collyers' mansion. Dilapidation of the structure had led to instability. Once the debris removal had started, the building officials deemed it too dangerous and called in large excavation equipment to bring down the structure and remove the debris. The Collyers' mansion did not have utility service, as over time the property had become in disrepair, bills became overdue and the city disconnected their utilities. Perhaps the biggest learning point from the Collyers' mansion conditions is the fact that the brothers no longer used the front door as an entrance. Their collection had taken over the space and made it impassable.

Each of these factors can be seen today and are very common. Taking these learning points from the historical case of the Collyers' mansion is essential to understanding the risks associated with a building that is overloaded with belongings.

Now that you know what Compulsive Hoarding Disorder is, it's time to learn more about the dangers that this amount of stuff can pose to a first responder. In the next chapter we will be looking into the dangers presented by hoarding and why it is important to understand these risks.

CHAPTER 3:
DANGERS TO FIREFIGHTERS

As the piles grow, so grows the danger to first responders. From access issues to fire load, the first responders tasked with entering a hoarding environment will be met with a plethora of challenges that must be adjusted for as they carry out the mission to protect life and property.

Fighting fires is an inherently dangerous profession that is further complicated when hoarding conditions are present. One of the greatest risks to firefighters is the collection of belongings that can be hidden behind closed windows, overgrown hedges, and other methods of concealment that keep the interior conditions of the home unknown until entry is made.

An occupant in this situation is termed a "Hidden Hoarder," meaning that the condition of the interior is hidden and not seen from the exterior. As noted earlier, with the afflicted person possibly being a recluse, he will often feel embarrassed and ashamed of his collection and will go to extremes to conceal it, hiding the condition until an emergency occurs. With reclusion and the hiding of the true condition of the building's interior, it is common for first responders answering a call for service to be the first to discover hoarding conditions.

Within the "Hidden Hoarder's" home, the interior conditions can be extremely dangerous to firefighters as they make an attempt to rescue a person or make the push on the fire. Falling debris, blocked secondary means of exit, and hidden pockets of fire can all be concealed until the firefighter exposes them. In the case of hidden fire, the firefighter can be exposed to a greater risk of rapid fire progression such as a flashover or backdraft (Taylor, 2007).

Flashover: Heat from the growing fire is absorbed into the upper walls and contents of the room. This heats up the combustible gases and furnishings to their auto-ignition temperature. Flashover is the sudden ignition of a room's contents into flames.

Backdraft: A phenomenon in which a fire that has consumed all available oxygen suddenly explodes when more oxygen is made available.

The compartmentalizing of rooms full of belongings is often found in hoarding, creating a compartment within a room. Imagine a home with hoarding conditions where access paths to the interior rooms are blocked by stacks of clutter. These blockages create walls of debris that can result in a sealed "room within a room". Essentially, this is a compartment where fire is able to hide for longer periods of time.

(Figure 3-1: Firefighters can be exposed to hidden pockets of fire deep within the stacks of stuff. In this picture FDNY firefighters battle a Heavy Content fire in Brooklyn. Photo Credit Lloyd Mitchell)

Hoarding also provides

hidden pockets of air for fire to hide in throughout a home (Figure 3-1). As the belongings stack up, the home becomes a series of these sealed containers. If a fire were to occur, it could stay small for a longer period of time due to the lack of airflow available. A small, smoldering fire can stay hidden for hours, allowing the heat to build to backdraft levels.

If the fire has a heat source coupled with lots of available fuel (commonly found in a hoarder's dwelling), the only thing it needs is oxygen. Air can be provided by incoming firefighters, thus exposing them to a rapid fire development event. If one of these events were to occur, the firefighter would be placed in significantly increased danger due to the lack of secondary means of egress due to windows and doors being blocked by the collection of stuff. Having these means of egress blocked requires the firefighter to exit using the same path of travel used to enter the room. The retreat could be further complicated by things that were knocked over as the firefighters entered the building (Taylor, 2007).

Insulating Characteristics of Hoarding

Hoarding a variety of belongings until the stacks reach above waist level can present a unique challenge to firefighters, and yet at the same time offer a layer of survivability to trapped occupants. Shielding the person inside the pathways is a characteristic of hoarding conditions and can offer a false sense of security for firefighters making an interior fire attack (Project Kill the Flashover, 2015).

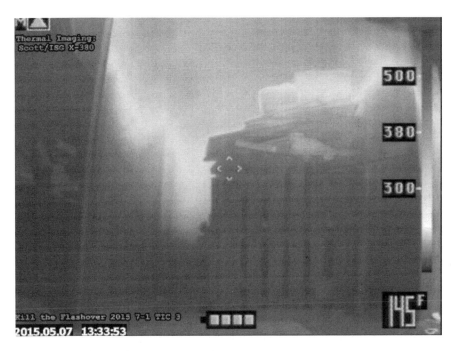

(Figure 3-2: Thermal imagine picture from KTF Burn 7-1 showing the shielding effects of the Hoard. In this picture you can see the nozzle of advancing firefighters on KTF 2015 burn 7-1. Photo Credit Project Kill The Flashover)

Firefighters progressing into an interior structural firefight must use all five senses to determine the conditions. If the firefighter is crawling through stacks of stuff at or above waist level, the belongings can shield the firefighter from the true conditions. Floor temperatures are often in the 100-150° temperature range, while the ceiling and other parts of the room climb above 350°, the temperature required to start breaking down the face piece of an SCBA (Figure 3-2).

If the advancing firefighters do not rely on their senses to develop a good situational awareness of the fire conditions due to the hoarding, they may be lulled into a false sense of safety and continue to advance deeper into the structure. If the fire reaches rollover and flashover conditions, the firefighters may find themselves in a situation where they have no escape route. Remember, hoarding vastly increases the fire load of the structure.

When entering a hoarder environment, the use of a thermal imaging camera (TIC) should be a standard procedure in order to allow the crew to assess the ceiling and floor temperatures. Seeing ceiling temperatures above the 300-600° range should alert the crew to be wary about advancing into the structure, as in most cases hoarding limits the available primary and secondary escape routes. Caution should be taken to ensure the interior crews are not being exposed to rapid fire growth and entrapment (Figure 3-3).

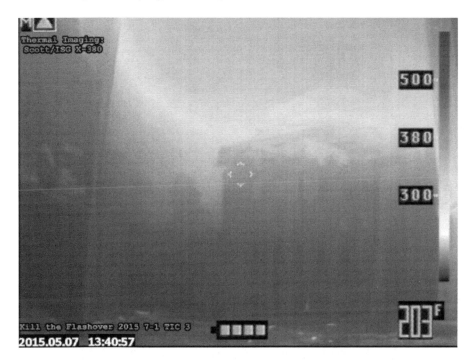

(Figure 3-3: Firefighters crawling between the stacks of stuff and walls reported minimal heat. In this pictures firefighters advance down the hallway into simulated Heavy Content Conditions during Kill the Flashover 2015, Photo Credit Project Kill the Flashover 2015)

On the upside, interior firefighters can use the stacks for shielding when attacking the ceiling. As firefighters prepare for the indirect attack of the fire, they can use a "dig in" approach to create a barrier between them and the disruption in the thermal layering that will result from attacking the fire and cooling the environment. Approaching the stacks and remaining close to them can shield the firefighter from the heat felt during fire attack.

Shielding effects created by heavy contents will also help protect trapped victims. Occupants found deep inside the pathways between stacks of belongings will have additional shielding from high heat temperatures. This shielding action offers a greater chance of protecting the occupants from the thermal dangers of the fire. Tightly packed belongings can shield the floor area and provide temperatures in the 100-150° range. At these levels a person can survive for extended periods of time, assuming that the byproducts of combustion don't kill them first. Carbon monoxide and hydrogen cyanide are examples of such byproducts.

If the occupant has the right ventilation or access to pockets of air, the shielding can keep him alive for a longer period of time. Keeping this variable in mind when making a victim survivability profile can lead firefighters to stay in rescue mode longer before switching to recovery mode. However, with this in mind, the firefighter must search all around to find occupants trapped in these areas of refuge.

Debris

Another danger to firefighters in hoarding conditions is debris that can strike, block, or slow a firefighter entering the building. The collection itself can be a huge danger to firefighters making an attack or attempting a rescue. This danger can reach far beyond the walls of the building. The yards of compulsive hoarders often have massive amounts of belongings that hamper access to even begin the firefight.

Fall hazards are another major concern for firefighters dealing with the stacks of belongings. While it is common for firefighters to crawl into burning buildings, stacks of collected materials can force crawling firefighters to stand up to maneuver around or over the stacks. Forcing firefighters to stand up exposes them to a greater risk of heat exposure and an even greater risk of injuries from a fall. Standing also raises the firefighter's center of gravity higher from the floor, and many items found in the stacks, such as magazines, books, and cardboard, can be very slippery when exposed to the water from hose lines.

The paths through the debris often present in hoarding conditions are called "goat paths" (Bratiotis, et al., 2011). While making it easier for firefighters performing a search to find a trapped victim, goat paths can offer challenges. Maneuvering through them can be tricky because they are intended for a person to walk through without wearing turnout gear and SCBA (Figure 3-4). As firefighters make their way through, stuff can fall and strike the firefighters and/or block their pathway out. Again, a TIC is one of the essential tools used for search and rescue operations within these types of dwellings.

(Figure 3-4: Firefighters using pathways to search a simulated Heavy Contents area. In this picture firefighters from Saint Albans WV drill inside Heavy Content Conditions. Photo Credit Author)

As a general rule of thumb, firefighters should try to avoid climbing over piles of belongings until the contents can be identified. In smoke-filled environments, making the determination between stacks of books or stacks of glasses can be difficult. Once the smoke conditions improve, this identification becomes easier. Firefighters, weighted down from their gear, can cause stacks of glasses, cardboard, and many other items to collapse, creating the potential for injury and/or entrapment to the firefighter. Using the goat paths around the hoarder's belongings is a best practice when entering these environments.

Occupant Dangers

Interacting with the occupants of a Compulsive Hoarding Disorder environment can be a challenging situation. Remembering the complexity of the disorder, responders need to be understanding of the occupant's attachment to the belongings. Responders cannot be judgmental to this attachment. If an environment is trashy, smelly, and nasty, responders cannot tell the occupant how nasty or smelly or trashy it is.

Remember, these folks have a compulsion to collect that is a diagnosable psychological disorder. As their stuff grows, their attachment grows with it. This is where the need for understanding comes in. Occupants must be treated respectfully and with understanding. Derogatory terms should not be used when operating around the occupant. Most who suffer from Compulsive Hoarding Disorder view the word "hoarder" as a derogatory term. More appropriate terminology should be used when describing the condition of the building.

Other terms used around the world are "packrat conditions", "trash house" and "lasagna house". All of these terms can be viewed by the occupant as derogatory. Instead of using these types of terms, the term "heavy content environment" (covered in an upcoming chapter) should be used.

Mimicking the terminology of the occupant will lower the risk of being offensive. If the occupant calls his stuff a collection, or belongings, use that term when interacting. Can firefighters do this in a life-threatening situation? The answer would be no. Firefighters cannot take the time to explain or interact with the occupant if they are inside a burning building in need of rescue. Can firefighters be mindful while performing life saving measures? Yes, but life safety will always be the most important priority. Most often, responders will be dealing with occupants in non-life threatening situations such as a medical emergency.

Imagine you are tasked with entering one of these

environments for a medical emergency and you need to interact with the occupant. You want to be respectful when interacting. "Mr. or Mrs. Johnson, I understand these are your belongings, but we need to move them to get you out of here". This is where some of the problems can occur due to the compulsion.

Often the occupant will feel threatened and won't want you touching his belongings. Now, you're asking yourself, 'How could we ever enter these environments without touching some of the stuff?' That's where responders should interact with occupant by saying, "Mr. or Mrs. Johnson, I apologize for knocking over your stacks of stuff. It's just a little tight getting in here. I will pick it up and move it over". Using this interaction technique will show understanding during the occupant treatment process.

The compulsion to protect belongings can compel the occupant to return to a burning building. Multiple cases have been documented where the occupant has self-extricated from the house on fire and run back in trying to save his perceived treasures. A first arriving fire crew must be aware of this possibility and ensure the safety of the occupant. Utilizing bystanders, EMS, or law enforcement to monitor the occupant will free first arriving firefighters to focus on battling the fire.

One particular case that stands out is out of Philadelphia, Pennsylvania, where the occupant of the building ran into the home multiple times from the porch of his middle-of-the-road townhouse. He successfully made it out two times, but the third time he was unable to escape and perished in the fire. This illustrates how strong the compulsion to protect belongings can be. When interacting with an occupant in a life-threatening or an active fire situation, physical restraint may be required to secure the safety of the occupant (Whelan, 2014).

Firefighters need to be aware of all radio communications (Figure 3-5). An example of this would be an interior firefighter communicating with the exterior commander. "Interior attack to command, this is a hoarder house." This communication can be easily overheard by the occupant and can cause emotional harm or even lead to physical harm. Firefighters need to understand the stress the occupant is experiencing while watching the perceived treasures burn. Adding to the stress by using derogatory terms such as "hoarder" could overwhelm the occupant and push him to violence.

Firefighters also need to be mindful that the occupant interaction continues all the way through the fire-ground. Just because the fire has been extinguished does not relieve firefighters of the responsibility to be respectful in both actions and communications. The overhaul process can be the most stressful time for the occupant. Watching the removal and discarding of belongings may also trigger emotional, if not violent, reactions. Understanding the attachment, responders should take the time to explain the overhaul process. Explaining the process and reassuring the occupant of the intent to salvage his belongings can ease some of the pain the occupant is experiencing.

(Figure 3-5: Firefighters should use Non-Offensive language over the portable radios. Here, Fire Chief Dave Wagoner,

Pinch VFD, uses his portable during 1403 burn prep. Photo Credit Author)

Think for a minute if you were an occupant of a home where you see firefighters picking up shovels full of gold bricks and throwing them out the window. What would your reaction be? This is an illustration of the reaction occupants can have if they see their perceived treasures thrown around. If the occupant is still on scene, he may need to be removed from the vantage point where he can see his personal belongings being removed by firefighters. If the occupant is unwilling to cooperate, removal from the scene may be required. Law enforcement should be utilized to ensure that all local laws are followed.

Interacting with the afflicted occupant can be a challenging and potentially dangerous situation. Using a non-aggressive, understanding approach can lead to a successful interaction with the occupant. The occupant will adjust for the blocked entrances, and even use exterior scaffolding and ladders to access second story living spaces once the first floor has become full of belongings.

Blocked Entrances and Exits

Adding to the dangers when faced with hoarding conditions are the blocked entrances and exits that the occupant does not use. It is common in hoarding conditions for the occupant to not use the usual means of entrance and exit. Once the accumulation of belongings takes over the rooms where the front or back door are located, the occupant will seal them off and use an alternative means of entering, such as a window or a garage door.

Arriving on the scene of an emergency without knowing that the usual access points are blocked poses an increased risk to firefighters. Wasting time trying to force a door that has stacks of stuff behind it can delay the rescue of a trapped occupant while giving the fire a chance to intensify and spread. Once a home or building with a hoarding condition has been discovered, the Pre-Fire Plan needs to identify the occupant's primary means of entry and exit.

Upon discovery of these conditions, an interview with the occupant or the neighbors can help evaluate the points of entry used by the occupant. There are also cues and clues to identify the points of entry that will be covered in later chapters.

Collapse dangers

Hoarding conditions can stress a structure to its weight limit before the first drop of water has been added. The dangers of the sheer weight of the building due to years of collecting should be on the forefront of all responders' minds. The combination of weighted down structural members with the effects of rotting from exposure to water damage and other forms of dilapidation can cause the "perfect storm" for a collapse.

It is essential to add extended burn times as an additional variable to this "perfect storm." Hoarding can limit the amount of available air, thus keeping the fire smaller and hiding the burning from discovery. Burn times have been seen in excess of 12 hours in hoarding conditions. Imagine the structural damage that could be caused by a burning fire left undiscovered for 12 hours.

It is paramount that responding firefighters who discover hoarding conditions stay on high alert for potential structural collapse risks. Firefighters should remain outside the collapse zone until an accurate assessment of the risks has been completed during the 380° size-up, which will be detailed in Chapter Eight. During this assessment, the firefighters should double the estimated burn time. If the building is suspected to have been burning for 20 minutes, the estimate should immediately go to 40 minutes or more. Doubling this estimate allows firefighters to be in a defensive mindset and adds a layer of caution to their attack. Even after doubling the estimate, firefighters should be mindful of the potential for collapse.

Dilapidation Dangers

With large amounts of belongings comes an increased risk of structural damage caused by the associated loss of utilities, burst water lines, and lack of general upkeep needed to keep a home in good standing (Figure 3-7). Adding in the weight of the belongings creates a recipe for a disaster even before

the first drop of water has been applied.

(Figure 3-7: Heavy Content homes can show signs of collapse long before a fire occurs. Photo Credit Author)

At 8.33 pounds per gallon, how much water will be needed to bring a home piled with tons of debris to the ground? While the answer to this question may not be black and white, it should be at the top of the list of dangers considered by firefighters after making the discovery of hoarding. Remember the case of the Collyer brothers in NYC, where they removed over 136 tons of belongings and ultimately had to tear down the building because it became unstable once the belongings were removed (Frost, Steketee, 2010).

(Figure 3-8: Firefighters should use corners to help reduce collapse danger. Photo was taken during a 2-alarm fatal hoarding fire in Delaware County PA. Photo Credit Delaware County PA Fire Dept.)

The collapse risk should be kept in mind throughout all phases of the operation, including overhaul of the fire. In fact, the collapse risk should be evaluated at each point of transition during the firefight. Once the main body of fire has been knocked down, an inspection of the structural integrity throughout the entire building should be conducted.

Using hooks or poles to poke inspection holes or pull ceilings down is imperative to determine the depth of burn damage. Multiple inspection holes are needed in each room of involvement and surrounding the fire room.

In order to offer a buffer zone of safety for on-scene personnel who suspect a collapse is imminent, all firefighters and apparatus should be removed from the collapse zone and placed in the corners as these are areas of safety in the event of a collapse (Dunn,1992) (Figure3-8). A master stream attack should also be used. In some cases an excavator may be needed to begin tearing down the structure prior to applying water to the fire.

Structural problems caused by water damage,

including mold and rot, can go unnoticed due to debris hiding the damage. The potential for mold can expose the unsuspecting responder to inhalation dangers when running a medical or automatic fire alarm. Responders entering a hoarder home should consider respiratory protection such as a N95 Respirator, which is approved for dusts, fumes, mists, and microbial agents.

Electrical fires are one of the most common types of fires in hoarding conditions. From broken electrical wires to overloaded individual outlets, the dangers are numerous. If a spark were to occur, the outlet is often in close proximity to a stack of combustible materials such as newspapers or books. This danger can be found throughout the entire home, not just in an attic or basement.

It is common to discover that the electricity of a hoarder home has been disconnected by the power company and the occupant is using alternate ways to obtain electricity. Generators, inverters, or extension cords run from nearby homes are all situations often found in homes where electricity has been disconnected.

This poses a serious risk to the firefighter who assumes that all electricity has been disconnected when it is discovered that the meter is missing. If the meter is missing and/or pulled in a home with hoarder conditions, further inspection is still warranted to make sure the electricity has been completely shut off.

Overstressed Dangers

By far, the biggest danger presented by hoarding conditions is the overwhelming workload that is placed on the first responders. From strains and sprains to heat emergencies, the men and women who respond to these emergencies face a workload that is drastically increased (Figure 3-9). With heart attack and stroke being the number one killer of firefighters, the over stressing of firefighters due to workload offers the biggest potential for injury or death of a firefighter. Hoarding can take the simplest task and turn it into a labor intensive job that requires additional staffing to complete.

Understanding this potential for a disaster incident, commanders must make adjustments when the discovery of hoarding conditions is made. Having the needed additional responders on the scene to carry out the necessary tasks requires that a decision be made early in the response. Calling additional responders in early and returning them if not needed is a much better option than needing their help and having to wait for them to respond to the scene.

When dealing with this increased workload, extra time is required to allow proper rehabilitation for the working firefighters. Proper rehab is essential to lower the risks of heart attack and stroke. If sufficient rehab is not allowed, the work stress placed on the firefighters may be enough to cause an event. Cycling firefighters with shorter work times and longer rehab times is essential to keeping everyone safe.

(Figure 3-9: Firefighters will experience a higher volume of work during a heavy content fire. In this picture, Detroit, Michigan firefighters pulling hose during a 2-alarm commercial heavy content fire. Photo Credit Lloyd Mitchell)

Biological Dangers to First Responders

The biggest risk to first responders for non-fire related responses is the exposure to biological hazards. Human to human or animal to human exposures can become the greatest danger when responding to a non-fire emergency. Exposure to these conditions often occurs because personal protective equipment (PPE), such as respiratory protection, is not used. Many first responders are familiar with the "ammonia" smell, but few have understood just how dangerous conditions such as exposure to increased levels of ammonia can be.

In hoarding conditions, it is common to find multiple animals of different types in the home. Large numbers of cats, dogs, ferrets, or birds contribute to the risks of exposure to the non-protected first responder. The presence of stacks of belongings also brings an increased risk of exposure to mice and insects that cannot be controlled due to the limited access to all parts of the home. Viruses such as the Hantavirus, which is rodent-borne, can often be found in hoarding conditions.

Hantavirus Pulmonary Syndrome (HPS) is a severe and sometimes fatal respiratory disease in humans caused by infection with a Hantavirus. Anyone who comes into contact with rodents that carry Hantavirus is at risk for HPS. Rodent infestation in and around a home presents the risk for Hantavirus exposure. Even healthy individuals are at risk for HPS infection if exposed to the virus (CDC, 2014)

Primary animal to human exposure concerns:
- Tapeworm
- Hantavirus
- Psittacosis
- Cat Scratch Disease

These are some of the human to human exposure concerns:
- Listeria
- Hepatitis A and B
- Scabies
- Pneumonia
- Herpes Zoster virus

Responders must consider the different types of dangers presented from heavy content when choosing tactics, selecting levels of PPE, and make sound risk versus reward assessments. Some of these dangers are obvious, while others are rarely considered. Dangers presented can range from immediate life threats to a lingering chronic illness with effects can be seen for months. Recognizing and mitigating these variables is essential to protect responders and carry out the mission.

CHAPTER 4:
HOARDING AND THE FIRE SERVICE

Historically, dealing with hoarding conditions hasn't been studied or trained for in any great detail by Emergency Services. Since the days of the Collyer brothers, the fire service has simply dealt with these conditions as they occur and relied on plain luck too many times. Moving forward to the next generation of firefighters, there will be a need to study these fires, as they are far from "normal" or "routine". Hoarder homes can expose firefighters to increased numbers of risks not normally seen in uncluttered conditions.

The only published research on fires in hoarding conditions was produced in a joint project between the Worchester Polytechnic Institute and the Melbourne, Australia Fire Department in 2009. They surveyed Melbourne's run data for ten years and published some amazing statistics (Lucini, G., Monk, I., & Szlatenyi, C., 2009):

- Hoarding was present in only 0.25% of fires (48 fires).
- Hoarding contributed to 24% of preventable fire fatalities.
- Fires were contained to the room of origin in "normal" fires 90% of the time.
- Fires were contained to the room of origin in hoarding fires 40% of the time.
- Hoarding fires required an average 2.6 pumpers and 17.1 personnel.
- Routine fires required an average 1.5 pumpers and 7.7 personnel.
- Estimated damages to a home in "normal" conditions totaled $12,500.
- Estimated average damages to a home in hoarding conditions totaled $100,000.
- Cost to the fire department per fire was estimated at $2,100 for a "normal" fire.
- Cost rose to $34,000 in a hoarding environment.
- Only 26% of hoarder homes had working smoke alarms, compared to 66% in "normal" homes.

These statistics show that fighting fires in hoarding conditions costs more, requires more personnel, results in higher cost to the fire departments, and produces higher fire losses. The one staggering finding is that only 0.25% of their structure fires produced 24% of the preventable fire deaths.

Out of the 24% of fire deaths related to hoarding, the most important characteristic to note is the absence of working smoke detectors. This may be attributed to the lack of maintenance to a home as a compulsive hoarder's collection accumulates or the compulsion to keep the interior conditions secret. The saddest part of this statistic is that the lack of smoke detectors is one of the leading causes of death in non-hoarding fires. This tells us, as firefighters, that our role in fire prevention is not done, and that we must continue to strive to help prevent these senseless tragedies.

Hoarding Fires Are Happening

For a fire department to just assume that there are no hoarding conditions in their district is a mindset that can lead to firefighter fatalities. As mentioned in an earlier chapter, hoarding is not limited by borders, economic levels, or ethnicity, and can be found in everyone's district.

Since beginning this research and reaching out to

fire departments around the world, the most used term to describe their experience with a hoarding fire conditions was "LUCKY." Phrases like, "We were lucky that ....," "Fortunately we ....," and "We just got lucky no one was killed," are sentiments that kept repeating themselves over and over. While first responders do get "lucky" during an unstable scene, firefighters should not be relying on luck as a safety tactic. Firefighters should assume that the dangers posed by hoarding are present everywhere, educate themselves on the dangers, and remain vigilant in searching for them.

It is unknown, for now, how often hoarding fires happen in North America, as no reporting system exists and no data collection has been done. The only reliable resources we have to identify the frequency of occurrence of hoarder fires are the various news agencies. As these fires occur, the media seems to gravitate to these situations due to the larger scale and longer responses. Unlike many "bread and butter" fires, hoarding can lead to extended operational periods. This amount of time allows news crews to arrive, set up, and capture the firefight on film.

During my research over the past six months, hoarder fires have been documented around North America, Australia, Europe, and South America. Each occurrence brought similar challenges as the firefighters battled the blazes. The number of injured or killed first responders is also unknown, as the reporting system does not currently account for "hoarding" or "clutter" variables.

While the true number of firefighters injured or killed by these conditions unknown, there have been firefighter deaths where cluttered conditions were a factor contributing to their deaths. While the clutter itself may not have caused the death, the inability of firefighters to escape a rapid fire phenomenon and structural collapse are examples of areas where hoarding could have contributed to firefighter fatalities.

Case Study

ChamberofHoarders.com

Elyria, Ohio

Event Date January 18, 2015

Working Structure Fire with Victim Trapped

Location: Skylark Court, Elyria, Ohio

Time 16:00 Hours

Around 16:00 hours on January 18, 2015, the Elyria, Ohio Fire Department was alerted to a house fire. The initial dispatch was directed to an industrial area with a large warehouse structure and the first arriving unit advised nothing showing. Updated dispatch information redirected the responding units to the correct address and also advised the responding chief of a confirmed occupant trapped. Dispatch also passed along information from the caller that the occupant was a "Hoarder" and that they could see visible flames.

Engine 3 arrived on scene with smoke showing throughout the structure, with the heaviest amounts seen from division 2. Engine 3 chose an offensive posture with a 1 3/4 sized line for primary search and fire control. Ladder 7 advised that the heaviest fire was on the division 2 side C, while Chief 3 instructed them to ventilate vertically. Rescue 31 was directed for occupant search and rescue. A supply line was established by Engine 4. An unknown unit advised Chief 3 of an awning that was compromised by fire with "a lot of trash underneath it".

Upon hearing that report, Chief 3 ordered an emergency manpower recall. Shortly thereafter Chief 3 was advised that fire was extending to the upper floors and roof. A transitional attack was used after the discovery of fire extension to the roof area. Chief 3 then requested a Mutual Aid Box Alarm System (MABAS) box alarm assignment 1341 to respond and stand by. The second due company advised they were unavailable due to another assignment. Chief 3 then advised that the box would be sufficient without them and requested the fire prevention and training officer to the scene.

Shortly after that transmission an unknown crew member advised the Chief of fire on side C, "coming through the vent hole". At the 20 minute mark Chief 3 described their operation as a "marginal offensive attack" with the crew having difficulty making entry and unable to locate the victim. Chief 3 was then advised of heavy fire in the awning area again. Additional units began to respond from the call back. At the 40 minute mark Chief 3 announced that they were going defensive due to the amount of stuff inside.

The above information was obtained from the command channel audio files.

Operational functions Overview

Initial alarm assignments chose an aggressive interior posture for search and fire control. These crews were met with hoarding conditions with pathways as means of traveling between rooms. Their initial tactical objective was to search the upstairs of the home, where they believed the occupant was located. What they found in the process of making entry to division 2 (the upstairs) is that it was full of belongings with no pathways. Upon this realization the crews began to use VES (vent-enter-search) procedures to gain access to the rooms via outside windows. During this process firefighters had to remove multiple trees to gain access to the windows. They chose the oriented search as the means of positive location management due to the walls being unusable for orientation.

    Firefighters also began to search on the first floor, where one truck company captain described conditions changing from moderate to severe in a shorter than normal time period. He also described the stacks being so high at one point that his "air pack was dragging the ceiling." With the combined efforts of fire control and search proving to be ineffective, Chief 3 ordered all firefighters out of the building and into a defensive posture.

    Once everyone was out of the structure Chief 3 requested an excavator to the scene for building demolition and to search for the occupant. They were able to locate the victim under debris on the first floor.

The victim had the house so full of belongings that she could no longer use the second floor and had retreated to the first floor for day-to-day living. Overhaul and building demolition continued for hours and the aftermath was beyond words.

Elyria Hoarding Fire Successes:

- Dispatch advised crews of Hoarding Conditions
- Strong Command presence
- Great communication from interior crews to command and back
- Interior crews minimized number of firefighters inside
- Basic Fire-ground functions were assigned and performed
- Additional firefighters called in quickly
- 20 minute updates and reports given and used
- Constant updates from around the structure
- Defensive operations initiated in a timely fashion
- Excavators called in

Elyria Opportunities

- Initiate a Pre-Plan Process (Building officials had visited home multiple times)
- Utilize Police, Fire, EMS, and utilities to locate and

identify Hoarding Conditions
- Initiate common terminology to describe conditions (Suggested "Heavy Content")

Conclusion

The fire that occurred in Elyria, Ohio is a remarkable case study of success. While the occupant was not saved, operations used sound fire-ground practices and aggressive procedures to contain the fire and perform a search. The risk versus reward model was constantly used and communication was effective during the entire operation.

One of the biggest learning points from this particular fire is the Incident Commander's methodology and control over the fire scene. By effectively communicating with the operational firefighters, everyone understood their assignments, performed accordingly, and came home safe. There are very few suggestions for improvement from an operational standpoint, but the opportunity lies in having a common reporting system that can lead to effective pre-fire planning.

CHAPTER 5:
HOW MUCH STUFF?

A common misconception of the interior conditions found in a hoarding situation is that the home will be completely full. Imagine how long it would take to fill a home to waist level. It would takes weeks, months, or even years to accumulate that amount of belongings. There are different assessment scales used to rate the severity of hoarding conditions. Scales vary from a 1-10 range to the one featured here in this book.

The Institute for Challenging Disorganization established a 1-5 rating scale. This assessment tool is very detailed and takes into account many variables:

Five Assessment Levels of Hoarding

LEVEL COLOR	LEVEL OF CLUTTER
GREEN	LOW
BLUE	GUARDED
YELLOW	ELEVATED
ORANGE	HIGH
RED	SEVERE

While this assessment scale is a powerful tool for mental health professionals, it does not cover all the needed variables used by first responders. Keeping with the 1-5 scale, for simplicity, the first responder rating scale for cluttered conditions was developed (Prince, T., 2003).

Fire Service Pre-Plan Assessment Scale for Heavy Content Environments
Parameters for Assessment

Structural Integrity	Sagging roof or bulging walls
	Noticeable water damage
	Areas with high levels of content
	Collapse
	Do not enter buildings
Accessibility	Exterior clutter
	Privacy fencing
	Blocked or locked gates
	Primary points of entry used by occupants
	Secondary means of Egress
Interior Layout	Areas used for sleeping
	Open areas
	Unusable rooms
	Rooms of refuge
Special Hazards	Hazmat
	Animal type and number
	Utility variance
	Out of normal situations

Additional Resources	Animal control
	Utility companies
	Demolition crews
	Refuse company
Apparatus Placement	Ladder placement
	Collapse zones
	Estimated exterior fire direction
	Large trees and vegetation
	Stretch lengths
	Attack points
PPE Levels (Non-Fire responses)	Respiratory protection
	Splash protection
	Decontamination level
	Ventilation level

Level 1 Heavy Content
Most homes that have fires are this level

Structural Integrity	All components intact (No noticeable dilapidation) No signs of overloading
Accessibility	No noticeable clutter on the exterior All fences are accessible Backyard is free of clutter 360° of building is accessible
Interior Layout	Occupants sleep in bedroom Living spaces have some noticeable clutter All exits are available All windows are available
Special Hazards	No additional hazards Utilities - normal connections 1 or 2 pets with sanitary conditions Can add any special situations
Additional Resources	No additional resources needed

	May need Child or Adult Protective Services
PPE Levels(Non-Fire responses)	Dust mask may be needed Normal BSI precautions

Level 2 Heavy Content
Build Phase

Structural Integrity	One or more blocked exits One or more windows blocked Minor cosmetic damage to exterior structure
Accessibility	Noticeable exterior clutter All sides of the exterior can be accessed No locked or blocked gates Secondary means of egress limited by clutter
Interior Layout	Sleep area (options may be reduced in number) One or more blocked entrances Rooms of Refuge Uncontrollable airflow Some pathways have been established
Special Hazards	2 or more family pets Exotic animals (snakes, alligators, etc.) Large number of power cords

	Fecal matter (Pet and Human)
Additional Resources	Animal control Clean up company Extra EMS to compensate for workload Extra alarm for manpower
PPE Levels(Non-Fire responses)	N95 or higher protection Boot covers Splash Protection Natural Ventilation

Level 3 Heavy Content
Big troubles in small spaces

Structural Integrity	Noticeable roof deterioration
Noticeable wall bulging
Porches in disrepair
Accessibility	Two or more exits blocked
Locked privacy fences and gates
Cluttered yard with pathways only
Ladder truck space reduced
Windows inaccessible from the outside
Interior Layout	Bedrooms completely full
Occupant sleeps near kitchen
Clutter near shoulder height
Pathways used for passage
Rooms of no-entry
Special Hazards	More than 5 house pets
Overloaded outlets
No running water
Mold visible

Additional Resources	Animal control
	Utility companies
	Extra alarm for manpower
	Increased EMS for Responders
PPE Levels(Non-Fire responses)	APR or higher minimum
	Positive or negative pressure ventilation
	Splash protection
	Patient gross decon before transport
	Equipment decon following call

Level 4 Heavy Content
Nearing the end

Structural Integrity	Obvious structural damage
Danger of collapse (Before water application)
Noticeable large levels of clutter
Accessibility	Yard blocked access to most spaces
Minimal outside pathways
Large amounts of debris in exterior
Most windows and doors are blocked
High privacy fencing
Interior Layout	Very few usable spaces
Sleeping spaces - small open spaces only
Most rooms are full
Clutter at or above shoulder height
NO ENTRY ROOMS
Usually only one point of entry and exit

Special Hazards	Large numbers of animals (pets and non-pets) Increased collapse risk No power meter Electric supply run from neighboring buildings
Additional Resources	Animal control Demolition companies Utility Companies Child or Adult Protective Services Triple staffing Double rehabilitation Increased EMS for Responders
PPE Levels(Non-Fire responses)	SCBA minimum Positive Pressure ventilation Splash Protection Requires gross decon Hospital fine decon

Level 5 Heavy Content
DO NOT ENTER

Structural Integrity	Major structural damage Areas of collapse Overloaded porches
Accessibility	Minimal access Requires long stretches Ladder not able to reach Limited access for hand lines
Interior Layout	NO USABLE SPACES All rooms are completely full Clutter is at head height or above Massive amounts of clutter
Special Hazards	NO ENTRY Collapse coming Stay out of collapse zones Increased risks for rapid fire behavior
Additional Resources	Demolition crew Extra alarm plus

	Additional EMS for crews
PPE Levels(Non-Fire responses)	NO entry Full encapsulation mandatory Decon mandatory **DO NOT ENTER**

This fire service version of the scale allows firefighters to assess the conditions and apply the needed changes for a safer response. Using the scale for pre-planning purposes will allow a commander to make informed decisions about the strategy he chooses by utilizing information obtained before the response.

One example would be a first arriving officer being made aware of a level 5 home that is no longer occupied and is so full of belongings that it would be impossible to safely remove a person. With this information the officer could choose a defensive posterior until the fire is knocked down and structural stability can be evaluated.

Knowing the condition of the building before the fire allows this decision to be made without risking any firefighters and is useful to help make informed decisions before the emergency.

CHAPTER 6:
HEAVY CONTENT - GIVING A NEW NAME TO HOARDING CONDITIONS

One of the most important variables in the response to a hoarding situation is identifying and clearly communicating that hoarding conditions are present. Around the world, first responders have different ways of communicating these conditions. While the conditions are the same, the terms used to describe them vary dependent upon the geographical location and/or experience with hoarding responses.

Some examples of terms used:
- Trash House
- Packrat Conditions
- Collyer's Mansion Conditions
- Hoarding or Hoarder House
- Overloaded House

Labeling the occupant's perceived mountain of treasures "trash," could cause a reaction that can easily place a first responder in danger. Afflicted persons can have such deep emotional attachment to their items that any thoughts of loss or disrespect could cause them to act out in the form of violence against the on-scene responders. It is not just the firefighter speaking with the occupant that must be mindful of this. Firefighters' radios can be loud, and if the occupant overhears something derogatory it could trigger a violent response.

Hearing these terms could agitate the occupant enough for him to cause physical harm to the responders. Firefighters are in the business of saving lives. While being sensitive to the situation, it should NEVER get in the way of this mission. Occupants should be treated like a firefighter would treat his mother, father, or other family member.

Treating this condition with respect and remembering that it is a disorder, not a choice, is often hard to do. While a collection of belongings can appear to be "trash" and have no apparent value, it is imperative that responders are not judgmental and understand that this disorder prevents the afflicted person from removing belongings. They <u>DO NOT</u> see their belongings as trash and do not want to be called a "hoarder" or a "pack rat." Would you?

A "Hoarder House" is another example of a derogatory term that can be perceived as offensive by the occupant. Most people who are afflicted are well aware of their disorder and take great lengths to protect their identity from the outside world. Even having responders at their home will cause a large amount of stress. Being described as a hoarder adds to this stress and can trigger a violent reaction. Changing this type of terminology in the fire service will be a monumental task. As Dr. Richard Gasaway has said, the only person that likes change is a "cold wet baby".

"Heavy content" was chosen for the kind nature of the term, its descriptive meaning, and most of all, to prompt the firefighter who hears those words broadcast in association with a response that they are in for a struggle. If someone hears this term and has never been exposed to these conditions, they should be able to determine the challenge without confusion.

The word "heavy" describes the sheer weight that has been added to the structure by the accumulation of belongings. Hearing the "heavy" part of this term should start the thought process into how long will it be before the building is pushed to collapse.

The word "content" describes what is causing the heaviness to the structure. It's these contents that can be the most deadly to first responders.

While it may not be a "Perfectly Politically Correct" term, it is as neutral as possible to signal everyone who hears it into thinking about its implications. Hearing this term will inform firefighters that hoarding is present so they can act accordingly to prepare for an increased risk of multiple dangers, the biggest being complete collapse.

Changing anything in the fire service takes time, effort, and support from many different directions. Use of the term "Heavy Content" will not be accepted by all, but it should be considered and implemented in all departments to both alert responders of the battle ahead and to ensure that occupants and their homes are referred to with respect.

To begin using this terminology, firefighters should first introduce it to the chiefs, training officers, and other responders that are in their own and other response districts. Introduce the term slowly with a full explanation of why it has been chosen. If people are forced into change, they will resist it. However, if the change is explained and they are helped to understand why this terminology, was chosen, they will be less likely to fight the change.

The term heavy content can also be applied to situations that are cluttered, but not by a compulsive hoarder. Some situations can cause severely cluttered circumstances without the presence of an afflicted person. An example of this situation is when multiple families reside in one home. This could be due to the loss of a job, divorce, or many other reasons. No matter what the cause moving multiple families into the same house can cause extremely cluttered conditions. Using the term pack rat, hoarder, or similar term in this situation would be incorrect. Choosing to use the heavy content term would be correct and would avoid the use of a derogatory term.

Essentially, the term "heavy content" could be used to describe a large amount of content, either inside or outside a structure. It can be applied to an overstocked warehouse, storage area, or any overloaded structure (Figure 6-1). Standardizing the terminology first responders use can keep everyone one the same operational page. By introducing this term to his department and surrounding areas, a firefighter will ensure the use, understanding, and the context of heavy content when broadcasting findings.

Using this standardized term will reduce confusion on the fire-ground when describing overload structures.

(Figure 6-1 Heavy content conditions can be found in commercial occupancies such as a Dollar Store. In this picture the Detroit Fire Department goes defensive on a well involved Family Dollar store where they encountered heavy content conditions. Photo Credit Lloyd Mitchell)

CHAPTER 7:
IDENTIFYING AND PRE-PLANNING HOARDER HOMES

Identifying and planning for responses in hoarder conditions can be a challenging undertaking. Many of these homes, stores, or mixed occupancies can be spotted with a slow drive-by assessment that easily identifies a heavy content condition is present. However, there are many times that the true interior conditions are unknown until firefighters make entry. Assessing a building for the cues and clues of hoarding should be included in all assessments, size-ups, and evaluations. While many clues will be big and glaring, some can be small and subtle.

Cues and Clues often seen in Hoarding:

- Overloaded front porches
- Covered windows

- Backyards full of belongings (often with a privacy fence);
- Hoarding in the car
- Overloaded detached and attached garages
- Overgrown hedges and vegetation blocking views into the structure
- Multiple non-functioning vehicles in driveway/yard
- Signs of multiple animals
- Multiple storage containers in yards

Having one or more of the above factors raises suspicions that a heavy content conditions are present and the inside is overloaded with belongings (Figure 7-1).

Overloaded front porches can be found at many homes where there are hoarding conditions present inside. In many cases these porches can be a window into the interior conditions. An example of this would be a home in a municipal area with building codes that prohibit the occupant from accumulating belongings on the front lawn. If the collection of stuff extends beyond the front porch the building inspector may come and levy fines or make the resident start the cleanup process. Most codes allow the collection to take up the entire front porch space.

Firefighters who find an overloaded porch must assume the inside looks the same way until confirmation has proven otherwise. If unable to see the interior of the home, a look into the back yard, windows, and other areas can gather the needed information to begin a pre-incident plan.

(Figure 7-1 Drive by assessments of buildings in your district can reveal cues and clues. This house has begun to show the effects of becoming full by storage in the outdoor spaces. Photo Credit Author)

Covered windows can be a confusing inspection obstacle. Many dangers can lay behind blocked windows, from meth labs to hoarding. Blocked ndows should be a huge reminder that something is off and not normal with the occupancy. If firefighters notice blocked windows before the fire occurs they can assess what is blocking them. Stacks of stuff, large furniture, or windows just covered in plastic will need to be assessed when noting hoarding conditions.

(Figure 7-2 Occupants can use different methods to conceal the contents in the back yards. In this photo the occupant has used overgrown shrubs and privacy fences to hide the belongings. Photo Credit Author)

Overloaded back yards are a constant finding with heavy content conditions in both municipal and rural areas. The same building codes that keep the clutter out of the front yard are absent in the back yard, making it the perfect spot for the overflowing amounts of belongings to accumulate (Figure 7-2). Commonly the occupant can either begin or continue his collection in outbuildings and backyards, often with high standing privacy fences concealing the contents.

Discovering whether the back yard is full of stuff can be a challenge if the responder has been called for another emergency situation. During a medical call or other public assist call, the inspection/pre-fire plan process can take place after patient care has been completed. If firefighters suspect, an occupant is hoarding in a back yard, commonly blocked by high privacy fencing, a great resource for inspecting this situation is Google Earth.

Google Earth is a great tool to use for carrying out building inspections. Getting a bird's eye view of the footprint, layout, and challenges around a building will allow the responders to have an accurate assessment of square footage, and in the case of high privacy fencing, it can get a close look at the presence of heavy content. If heavy content is present, Google Earth is able to zoom in close enough to assess what is being stored in a back yard, pathways available, and to identify dangers that may be faced.

Another option would be to print out the overhead

view of the property and add it to the pre-fire plan. Departments can incorporate these photos into a program highlighting points of access and areas of concern. Having them available will allow responding personnel to accesses it when determining the best routes of entry into the building. Using the pathways will be the safest and most effective way to gain access, and having a view of them will allow for quicker determination of the best routes.

It is common for persons with Compulsive Hoarding Disorder to use their vehicles to collect, and often store, belongings until they can transfer them to the interior of the building. Just like their homes, their cars can accumulate a large amount of stuff inside them. These cars may have stuff stacked as high as the windshield, with only enough room for the person to sit in order to drive the car (Figure 7-3).

No formal research has been found that relates the frequency of hoarding in cars to hoarding in homes, but if these conditions are found in the occupant's car, this necessitates a closer look at the home, as it is likely in the same condition.

Having multiple storage buildings and containers in the yard and driveway of a building is an additional common finding in properties with heavy content conditions. Often, the collection starts with the outbuildings until their capacity has been met. Once those are overflowing with belongings, the occupant may switch to plastic containers aligned with shelving covered by a roof or some type of covering to keep them out of the weather. It is common to see creative ways of collecting things in yards and outbuildings. During the collection of research for this book, one common finding was noted in all pictures submitted. Blue tarps were seen covering outside storage areas. Varying in sizes, each and every picture collected had a blue tarp in some capacity.

(Figure 7-3 Non-functioning vehicles often are used for storage containers. In this photo the occupant has filled this van full of content. Photo Credit Author.)

Much like covering the windows, occupants who are trying to hide their collections will allow the shrubbery and trees to grow until the property is shielded from the prying eyes they believe to be watching them. Finding a house that is completely covered may not be a sure-fire indication of its contents, but it will require the firefighter to dive deeper into its potential for hiding heavy content. The pre-planning stage is the best time to start this deeper look.

Using some of the techniques outlined in this book can better help firefighters identify suspected hoarding conditions. The best practice approach to pre-incident planning for hoarding is to have a common reporting system. Soliciting reports from EMS, police, and utility workers can increase the opportunity to identify hoarding conditions. A common form and reporting system must be shared between all of entities that are submitting reports. Heavy content poses dangers to each of these groups, and by working together to identify these conditions, it allows everyone to better prepare for an emergency inside a hoarder home.

Another great resource for identification of hoarding in an area is to involve third party EMS providers that transport patients for doctor's appointments, kidney dialysis, and other non-emergency calls. Asking them to call for "Lifting Assistance" or to request help in patient removal, even if they don't require the assistance, will give firefighters legal access to help the patient and begin the pre-plan process. Once the patient is loaded, firefighters can take some extra time to look around to search for complications related to hoarding.

Starting a pre-planning process in a fire district can be simple or complex depending on the level to which a firefighter wants to take it. Start with the form currently being used to plan a response to multi-family dwellings and/or target hazards. Using the same form will allow uniformity in reviewing the pre-plan while taking less time to identify the hazards when responding to these conditions. There will need to be some additions and adjustments to the form in order to identify all of the specific hazards associated with hoarding.

Mandatory information needed:
- Number of Occupants
- Unusable entrances and blocked exits
- Rooms inhabitable due to belongings
- Roof conditions
- Support wall conditions

- Utilities which are non-functioning
- Primary means of entrance and egress
- Secondary means of egress
- Electrical supply (power drop or extension cords)
- Hoarding Level (1-5)

Optional Information:
- Types of belongings (car parts, books, etc.)
- Nearest relative contact information
- Length of hose needed to reach all areas of house
- Levels of PPE needed for a non-fire response
- Contact information to nearest clean out company
- Contact information for excavation services

The most important part of any pre-fire plan is the number of occupants that could be inside the structure at any point of the day. The same holds true for a house full of belongings. Establishing the number of people living there, if any, will be the number one priority for the planning process. Finding the exact number of adults, children, and animals may be challenging as the resident does not usually offer this type of information due to the reclusion that often goes with the disorder.

It may not be possible to obtain an actual number, but responders should strive to determine the number of occupants permanently living or potentially living inside. By having this number, a first arriving officer can make sound, fact based decisions in the risk versus reward analysis. It is common for occupants to fill their home until they can no longer live there. Once completely full and un-inhabitable, they will have the utilities removed and move into a new occupancy without cleaning out the previous home.

Awareness of these conditions before the fire happens will allow the Officer in Charge (OIC) to make the determination of "do not enter" or use a more defensive approach to the building if there is only a "chance" of squatters. Not risking firefighters' lives is an easier decision if there is proof that the occupancy is abandoned.

After determining the number of occupants, pre-planning the primary means of entrance and egress should be established, as occupants often use windows, garage access, and unusual modes to enter and exit.

One of the more interesting cases showed an occupant who erected scaffolding around the exterior of the home because the inside was so cluttered the interior stairwell couldn't be used. Unable to throw the belongings away, the occupant used construction scaffolding and ladders to create an entrance point to the only place left in the home that could be inhabited, an upstairs bedroom. Having the scaffolding in place when the fire did happen made the fire department's job slightly easier. They didn't have to ladder the building, as the ladders were already there (Personal Communication, A. Arnold, Shepherdstown, WV Fire Dept., April 2015).

Without knowing that ladders and scaffolding were in place for occupants to use as a daily entrance, an arriving fire department would mistakenly think that it was in place for a construction project, not for daily use. This should hammer home the need for a pre-fire plan, as the OIC will be able to not put firefighters into the interior.

From the same case of hoarding came the situation of rooms that were totally impassable. During the inspection, identifying and determining the rooms that would not support occupants being inside them should be the number one hazard on your plan. As the hoarding levels progress, the chance for rooms to be full of belongings increases. Knowing this before a fire happens will allow the OIC to eliminate those rooms as possibilities for searching or interior firefighting.

Identifying these potential death traps will help direct firefighters to the spaces that can keep occupants safe. Even if the rooms needing to be searched are not main living spaces, they may be the only spaces that an occupant could use as a point of refuge. If a fire was to happen, escape to these rooms may be the occupants' only chance of survival. Knowing the rooms that are full will direct searching firefighters to them last for confirmation. As responders continue to enter these pre-planned areas for different non-fire emergencies they should have access to records to maintain the most accurate conditions.

How in depth a pre-fire plan will be is dependent on an individual department. Meeting the minimum criteria above would be a basic plan to begin. This information needs shared with the dispatch center and mutual and automatic aid companies to ensure awareness of the conditions.

A sample dispatch would sound like, "Dispatch to Engine One, Truck One, and all responding companies to 123 Main Street, you are responding to a 40x50 single family with Level 4 Heavy Contents." This announcement should put everyone at a heightened level of awareness, knowing the response will have hoarding conditions.

Gaining access to pre-plan these structures can be difficult for first responders. Most people who hoard do not want anyone to enter the premises, especially those who can have them cleaned out, such as first responders. Being creative is the best solution to this access issue.

Some examples of access opportunities are:
- Medical responses
- Automatic fire alarms
- Drive by assessments
- Requests from family members
- Community visits to install smoke alarms
- Reporting system for neighbors
- Yearly inspections of multi-family occupancies
- Family reporting
- Mental Health Professionals
- Police Department reporting
- Utility companies

Each of the above listed opportunities can help establish the presence of hoarding conditions and all should indicate the need for a pre-fire plan.

Pre-fire Planning Examples

Below is a super-simple layout of a Heavy Content home interior. The plans can be very basic like this example or go into great detail. Using the system currently in place will determine the detail of the depth of review.

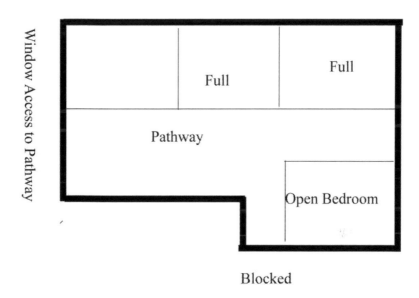

Blocked

CHAPTER 8:
380° SIZE-UP

Arriving on scene and determining the most appropriate actions necessary has long been accomplished with a standard walk-around the structure known as the 360° size-up. The additional 20° comes from an assessment of the occupant's vehicle. The 360° size-up requires a member of the first arriving company to walk around the structure and evaluate conditions, actions required, and the needs to accomplish these tasks. Without performing this complete assessment of the conditions, inappropriate tactics can be utilized.

When cluttered conditions are present, the need for this assessment increases. Establishing life safety hazards, points of entry and exit, fire conditions, and available airflow become more challenging when the access to the building is blocked with a large amount of debris. Many heavy content homes show no apparent signs of the interior status from the outside. The presence of these types of conditions is referred to as a "Hidden Hoarder." It may or may not be possible to determine the level of clutter inside before making entry, but there are many subtle cues and clues that can raise suspicion of heavy content.

A best practice in sizing up heavy content fires includes the pre-fire plan process covered in the earlier chapters. Establishing known, livable spaces and proper attack strategies before the fire happens is always the preferred way. The second step in the size-up is the dispatch.

Firefighters may suspect they are responding to a heavy content environment if the dispatcher makes statements such as, "Caller is advising the occupant is trapped inside by blocked exits." Or, "We are receiving reports the occupant is a hoarder." If these types of statements are transmitted during the dispatch or while responding, firefighters need to prepare for a heavy content environment.

As the apparatus approaches the scene it is essential for the first arriving officer to pull past the building if possible (Figure 8-1). Being able to see three of the four sides of the building from the street level allows the officer to assess the conditions.

During the first arrival and scanning of the three sides, firefighters should be looking for the following clues of a heavy content environment.

Overgrown vegetation
- Privacy fences
- Covered windows
- Cluttered front porches
- Stuff stored under tarps
- Multiple storage buildings
- Unusable cars packed full of contents

If any one of the above conditions is noticed, a further assessment for confirmation of clutter should be carried out. Finding more than one of the above variables raises the likelihood of finding a heavy content interior. Whether it is one or all of the above, firefighters should investigate further.

The amount of clutter visible from the street view can vary depending on rural or municipal districts. Cities have building codes and ordinances that will limit amounts of clutter that can be stored around the exterior of the building. Typically, the clutter in the front yard cannot extend beyond the front porch due to those regulations (Figure 8-1). Rural environments have no such regulations and cluttered front yards are common. Understanding the location of the building in relation to whether or not it is municipal or rural is essential due to the limitations of the building codes.

(Figure 8-1 Setting apparatus in a defensive position is inessential in heavy content condition in the event the fire spreads outside the building of origin. Delaware County PA firefighter showed great placement in this fatal heavy content fire. Photo Credit Delaware PA Fire.)

Both rural and municipal districts have some common findings (Figure 8-2). Regulations on the amount of clutter stored in the backyard are more relaxed than the front. This also is true for the side yards in the municipal districts. Using a privacy fence to surround the exterior of the home is common in both types of districts. Knowing that both types of districts allow for clutter around the building, firefighters should understand the importance of walking completely around the structure before choosing attack strategies and tasks. Firefighters who fail to walk completely around a structure could overlook the clutter and miss a huge indication of heavy content.

(Figure 8-2 Classic example of a Heavy Content exterior showing multiple clues. Photo Delaware County Pa)

Finding severely cluttered exteriors, while not being 100% accurate, is a great indication that the inside of the building may also cluttered (Figure 8-3). Exterior clutter is often the result of no usable space being available inside the building. As space becomes limited, the collection extends to the exterior of the building, often with multiple storage buildings, shelving, and stacks covered with blue tarps. These findings can make a complete walk-around assessment challenging (Figure 8-3). Utilizing available spaces such as pathways created by the occupant can make this assessment easier.

(Figure 8-3 Finding clutter around the exterior of a structure can give indications of the interior conditions. In this picture

Delaware County PA firefighters found exterior clutter and interior clutter. Photo Credit Delaware County Pa)

If a thermal imaging camera (TIC) is available, it is a best practice to use it during the initial walk-around assessment. Using a TIC allows firefighters to see escaping smoke, find the hottest part of the building, establish the coldest part of the building, and make more informed decisions. TICs give firefighters the ability to establish hot air exhaust around cracks and crevices found in the exterior of the building. Using the TIC to scan spaces that could be open, such as crawlspaces, attics, porch areas, and other areas that have the potential of being open will aid in the assessment of fire conditions.

Understanding the potential for discovery of ventilation-limited fires increases the importance of using a TIC. It is necessary to utilize tactical patience during this size-up in order to allow for more accurate attack strategies. Basic TIC use should be understood before using it for this process. TICs do have limitations and these limitations should be understood when applying the 380° size-up. An example of these limitations is the inability to see through glass windows. The TIC will see only the reflection off of the window and not through the window.

Once the apparatus has been placed and the TIC has been removed, firefighters should use a common starting point to begin their assessment to ensure that a complete walk-around has been accomplished. Cluttered conditions may prevent the starting point from being the address side, commonly referred to as side A. Wherever the start point may be, the key is to ensure a complete walk-around.

(Figure 8-4 Using the TIC during the 360° can identify hottest and coldest parts of the structure. In this picture a fire officer walks around KTF burn 7-1 to evaluate temperatures before entry, Photo Credit Project Kill the Flashover 2015)

During the 380° size-up firefighters, should be looking for the following indications of hoarding while evaluating:

- Blocked or locked entryways
- Covered windows
- Dilapidation concerns
- Uncommon points of entry (such as windows)
- Noticeable clutter in windows

(Figure 8-5 Looking for blocked windows is an indication of rooms that are impassible. In this picture the window of KTF Burn 7-1 is filled to capacity for burn testing, Photo Credit Author)

The above variables

should be added to the standardized walk-around assessment. If one or more of the above are found, a closer assessment of the interior is required. For example, while walking around the structure, a firefighter notices that two windows are covered with unusual types of coverings. This alone may not be an indication of heavy content conditions, but it does warrant further analysis. When seeing windows covered in an unusual way, firefighters should take the time to find a point of entry and look inside while keeping the amount of air added to a minimum.

During the 380° size-up of the heavy content environment, the extra 20° comes from an assessment of the occupant's vehicle. After discovering one or more cues or clues that indicate the potential for a cluttered environment, firefighters should take the time to look inside the occupant's vehicle. It is common to find that the vehicles are full of belongings. Discovering cars that are full of belongings is a clear indication that the interior of the building may also be cluttered.

Finding, or suspecting, the presence of heavy content should be communicated to all responding units quickly. Communication of these findings will allow commanders to make informed decisions on needed resources. Transmission of the findings in a timely matter also gives the mutual aid companies sufficient time to respond.

Here is an example of such a radio transmission: "Engine One to dispatch. Engine One is on scene of a single-family, single-story structure with a working fire. Engine One has its own water supply and will be using an offensive strategy. This is a heavy content environment." This announcement, whether right or wrong, informs all on-scene and responding personnel of the challenges that lay ahead. If things change and it is determined that heavy content is not present, firefighters can cancel the heavy content response and continue the operation as normal. Communication of the suspicion of heavy content does not affect operations but is rather an attempt to inform and forewarn.

During the 380 ° size-up, close attention to available spaces, fire dynamics, and flow path are essential. Fire requires heat, fuel, and oxygen to burn. Heavy content environments offer an unlimited amount of fuel, thus increasing the importance of air flow in and out of the building.

Establishing cold air intakes and hot air exhausts is vital. A well ventilated, heavy content environment is a challenging situation. Lack of control of the air combined with the unlimited amount of available fuel can allow fires to rapidly become uncontrolled. Establishing the amount of available air should be high on the priority list. If at any point during the 380° size-up an air track can be controlled, it should be done. An example of this would be taking the time to shut an exterior door or close an exterior window.

Controlling the available airflow during the 380° size-up can limit the fire spread, decrease fire size, allow additional time for hose advancement, and cool the environment by causing fire to go into decay.

The effects of air on heavy content fires was documented by the "Kill the Flashover" (KTF) project in 2015 (Figure 8-2). During testing in Shelby, North Carolina, the KTF project conducted three research burns in an acquired structure with heavy content conditions. Burn 7.1 was conducted in a ventilation-limited state. All windows and doors were in place and closed. Analysis of the thermal imaging data showed rapid fire growth from ignition and two temperature measurements in excess of 1200°. After reaching ceiling temperatures of 1200°, the fire in the room of origin began to see rapid temperature drop. Without available air, the fire burns itself down to approximately 180° (Project Kill the Flashover, 2015).

In comparison to KTF burn 7.1, 7.3 was conducted with multiple air tracks available. The resulting rapid fire growth and horizontal fire spread was a stark contrast to burn 7.1. Burn 7.3 progressed into all available rooms and quickly spread into the attic. Comparing these two research burns illustrates the importance of air track management. The old adage, "If you control the air you control the fire," is very applicable in a heavy content environment (Author Unknown).

(Figure 8-2 Having multiple air intakes can allow the fire to grow rapidly. In this picture firefighters from Project Kill the Flashover test a fire inside heavy content conditions with multiple flowpath's Photo credits Author)

The tactical 380° size-up is a continuation of the tried and true 360° size-up. To allow for the needed adjustments, all firefighters must recognize the cues and clues of a hoarded environment. It is the responsibility of all firefighters arriving on the scene to continually evaluate the conditions, actions, and needs. This responsibility does not end with the officer of the group, but it is shared by all firefighters. Adding the variables found in this chapter will allow firefighters to progress to the attack mode strategy and make a sound Risk versus Reward analysis of the structure.

CHAPTER 9:
RISK VS. REWARD

Fighting structural fires is an inherently dangerous job. All firefighters understand the danger and risks associated with performing this job under the most extreme circumstances on a day-to-day basis. It is the responsibility of all firefighters to minimize these risks and evaluate all practices to ensure that the risk that being taken is worth the reward they receive. Firefighters will utilize an extreme risk model to save a life. This model needs to be redefined to ask whether a life is savable. Determining whether the life is savable or not is more complex when dealing with hoarding situations, as multiple case studies have shown survival profiles to be different than when dealing with a non-cluttered environment.

A 2015 case study from Charles Town, West Virginia

is a great example of how different the variables can be. The Citizens Fire Company responded to a working structural fire in a residential structure with confirmed occupants trapped. First arriving fire crews found heavy fire conditions in the two-story wood-frame dwelling. Confirmation of three unaccounted-for occupants was received upon arrival of the first arriving crews. Two of the occupants were removed using ground ladders from Side C of the building. With the final occupant being unaccounted for, the Citizens Fire Company took on the risks associated with searching inside a cluttered environment.

Over a period of 31 minutes, the Citizens Fire Company worked diligently to locate the unaccounted-for occupant. First, a vent-enter-search operation was conducted on side C, division II of the structure. The interior crew was met with high heat, zero visibility, and an extreme amount of clutter. During the search they also located small pockets of available space where occupants could be located. After taking into consideration the length of the operation, the successful searches of the upstairs bedrooms, the downstairs fire conditions, the extreme cluttered conditions, and the survivability profile of the building, the Incident Commander announced the change from active rescue to recovery. Shortly after the transmission of these instructions the occupant was discovered on side D, division I (Pennington, 2015).

The Citizens Fire Company quickly removed the occupant to an awaiting ambulance for transport. The victim was severely burned, requiring extensive amounts of recovery time, but survived the fire.

(Figure 9-1 Adjusting the survival profile for heavy content fires may include increased chance of survival from the fire. In this picture the Citizens Fire Company performed two rescues from this heavy content home. Photo Credit Citizens Fire Company)

The diligent work, exhaustive efforts, and rational

thinking by the Citizens Fire Company led to the successful rescue of the occupant (Figure 9-1). During an interview with the Incident Commander, he stated that chances of a successful rescue were slim at the time of discovery. He described the amazement of the crew upon finding a live victim (Pennington, 2015).

The key variables in the successful rescue of this particular occupant were the shielding effects of the clutter found on top of her and her location in relation to an exterior window, which provided her with fresh air intake. She was found mostly covered by clutter and only a few feet away from an exterior window. The presence of these variables does not indicate extreme risks in all conditions; rather, they add to the set of variables used when conducting victim profiles. This case is also an excellent example of a situation where there is a transition from high risk to low risk procedures during the search process, as the victim was located by going through an exterior window, which places firefighters at low risk.

Identifying the risk

By reading this book, firefighters will better understand the challenges faced when dealing with fires in hoarding conditions. From the 380° size-up to the overhaul process, all of these risks are reviewed. When performing the initial risk versus reward analysis, firefighters should remember that overexertion of the initial crews can potentially be the most dangerous factor.

(Figure 9-2 Firefighters will be pushed to their physical limits when operating in heavy content conditions. In this picture firefighters from South Charleston and Dunbar WV take extra time to recover before entering a building for training evolutions. Photo Credit Author)

Crawling around, pushing over, cutting through, and dealing with the amount of clutter can push firefighters to their physical limits. The Incident

Commander must understand the crew's physical abilities and limitations and plan for sufficient rehab during the initial assessment.

The physical stress and environmental factors are two variables in the evaluation of the risk (figure 9-2). The potential for structural collapse, reviewed in Chapter Three, is another variable to consider. Ongoing evaluation of other variables present at an incident must occur throughout the course of the fire.

Evaluation of Risk

Upon discovery of a dangerous situation, the evaluation of how much risk to take should be completed. Life safety of the responders and the occupants of the building is the most important consideration. Variables such as known occupants trapped versus all occupants being out of the structure are the first indications of how much risk firefighter should take. Even if confirmation of trapped occupants is established, minimizing the risks is essential for firefighters. This can be accomplished through multiple tactics.

Evaluation of risks may include:
- Structural stability

- Known location of the victim
- Fire conditions
- Available resources
- Water supply
- Control of the air

Each of the above variables has increased importance in hoarding situations, especially for the first arriving companies. Firefighters should not take extreme risks to save a cluttered home or an unsavable life. If fire conditions dictate a defensive posture, firefighters should stay outside of the collapse zone and operate defensively until hazards have been sufficiently reduced. If a savable life is indicated, the same diligence should be taken during the rescue process period.

Prioritizing

During the risk versus reward assessment, the first arriving company should evaluate which procedures can positively influence the outcome of the operations with an acceptable level of risk. These operations include fire attack, aggressive search operations, and containing the fire to the structure of origin. The priority of operations that should be performed should be determined while continually evaluating all present risks. Once the goals have been established, they must also be continually evaluated for changing conditions.

Examples of changing risks requiring re-evaluation are rapidly increasing fire volume, confirmation the victim has been removed, loss of water supply, and discovery of clutter so extreme that firefighters should immediately leave the structure. The prioritization of operations should also allow for communications from all firefighters on the scene. This communication should be immediate during the evaluation of interior and exterior conditions, such as an Incident Commander noticing signs of a structural compromise and communicating this to the interior crew so they can quickly retreat.

Control

One of the potentially most challenging factors in calculating risk versus benefit in a hoarding situation is control of the firefighters. They are often aggressive by nature and will work themselves to exhaustion, placing themselves at great risk for the lives of others. Incident Commanders and firefighters must approach hoarding situations with extra control. The conditions present at each fire dictate how aggressive the tactics should be.

One of the most difficult situations a firefighter can face is the confirmation of a trapped occupant inside a structure where clutter conditions and fire volume dictate a no-go assessment. In this situation, the risk may outweigh the reward. A Michigan firefighter, who wishes to remain anonymous, shared a story where his fire department arrived on the scene of a two-story structure with a confirmed victim trapped and a large volume of fire. He witnessed multiple firefighters disregarding direct commands from their officers as they attempted to make entry to save the occupant (Anonymous, 2013).

Controlling of on-scene personnel should be accomplished by the use of open-ended explanations of the conditions. This can reduce the amount of stress felt by the firefighters unable to accomplish the rescue. For example, "Command to all on scene personnel - we are switching to a defensive posture until fire volume and environment control can be maintained". While using open ended communication does not eliminate the potential for rescue, it explains the conditions and actions needed in order to progress to the operation of removal of the occupant.

CHAPTER 10:
OFFENSIVE OPERATIONS

Upon discovering that heavy content conditions are present within a structure, firefighters should not automatically assume a defensive attack is the only strategy available to fight the fire. The final determination as to the type of fire attack will be dictated by any pre-incident intelligence, size-up information, and resources available. Firefighters can make entry into a heavy content environment (and have been doing so for many years) with varied levels of success. As a successful offensive attack poses challenges and an increased risk to firefighters, it is necessary to understand the many adjustments needed for a safe operation. Choosing the proper points of entry, attack method, and additional crew size needed can increase the likelihood of a successful fire suppression operation.

Go or No-Go Determination

Following the tactical 380° size-up, firefighters should evaluate the newly acquired information to make a go or no-go determination before entering a heavy content environment. For the purpose of this chapter, assume that all indications are present for an interior operation. Whether it is for an attempted rescue or fire control, the decision to operate inside the building must be made. Before making entry, a solid go/no-go assessment should be made at the point of entry. The go or no-go determination is based on many different variables. Even if the variables indicate a go, this does not relieve firefighters of the responsibility to use constant situational awareness and monitor conditions, as they will change.

GO

Many different variables found during the initial assessment will indicate a go. It is vital for firefighters to make an accurate assessment before entry (Figure 10-1).

These variables include a thermal imaging reading of 400° or less. Scanning the entry point with the thermal imaging camera can provide an accurate indication of the conditions through the smoke. The

scan should begin below the neutral plane. This allows the firefighter to see the conditions of the room. *(Figure 10-1 Firefighter making entry through a smoke curtain. Photo from KTF 2015 Burn 7-1, Photo Credit Jeff Harkey)*

During this evaluation below the neutral plane, the firefighter should be looking for the cluttered conditions, pathways, cold spaces, and air intakes. The best time to accomplish the scan will be shortly after the door is opened. In the first seconds after opening, the smoke will lift and provide better assessment below the neutral point. Beginning the TIC scan low in the colder area will allow the camera to stay in the higher resolution mode due to the lower temperature. Doing the bottom up scan is away from traditionally taught methods. If firefighters begin the scan near the top firefighters should pay close attention to the color palette of the camera to ensure an accurate temperature assessment when scanning high to low. Sufficient time should be allowed for the TIC to adjust for the cooler environment.

Once the underside of the scan has been processed, moving the thermal imaging camera to the 48 inch mark from the floor will give an indication of how tenable it is for firefighters to enter. A temperature of 400° or higher around the 48 inches mark is a no-go. This temperature was derived from the capabilities of the modern firefighter PPE (Starnes, A., 2011). Firefighters will not be able to withstand temperatures above this, as it is the top end of the spectrum. Research has shown that it takes minutes to heat the room from 0° to 400°, while it takes only seconds to progress from 400° to flashover (Taylor, 2007). Finding a temperature above 400° at the 48 inch mark is an indication of a fire still growing and methods of fire control must be accomplished before crews enter. It is essential for firefighters to read the entire palette of color on the TIC screen not just the spot temperature.

Methods of lowering this temperature include closing air intakes, applying water to cool, and isolating the room if possible. Closing windows, hanging smoke curtains, applying water for cooling, and applying water through exterior walls are all options. If the no-go assessment is reached, another option would be utilizing a different point of entry, possibly working further away from the seat of the fire.

NO-GO

The determination to no-go would include all of the variables seen above. Temperature readings above 400° at 48 inches, a neutral plane that is still growing towards the floor, and uncontrolled air intakes feeding the fire stand out as the most important factors (Starnes, A., 2011). Adding to these variables, no-go assessments should also consider the absence of safety measures for interior firefighters. Examples of these safety measures include blocked secondary means of egress, no available backup hose teams, and extended response times for next arriving companies.

Finding one or more of the above-mentioned variables should indicate a no-go situation. Firefighters making a no-go assessment should not give up on the process of turning it to a go decision. Instituting solutions to control the environment and providing safety measures can be accomplished if firefighters work in an organized fashion to carry out the mission. Adequate staffing will increase the speed of these interventions. Firefighters should make every effort to use the outside in approach if victims are unaccounted for, as done in the Charlestown, West Virginia case (Pennington, 2015).

At some point during the operation, firefighters will have to enter the building to complete the extinguishment process or recover the victim, unless officers in charge choose to demolish the building. Understanding that firefighters will eventually have to get inside, all efforts should be made to control the environment and work towards this goal.

Point of entry

Once the size-up is over and the decision to go interior has been made, the point of attack should be made with a few variables in mind:
- How do the occupants enter and exit the structure?
- Obstructions around the exterior of the building
- Potential challenges for the hose teams

Determining the points of entry used by the

occupants will allow firefighters to use the existing pathways for entry. A key point to remember is buildings with heavy content can become so full with belongings that the "normal" entry points may be blocked and unusable. As noted in prior chapters, it's common for occupants to use windows, doors, ladders, or other means of entry once the house becomes full. Doing a good 380 ° size-up will help assist in identifying the most appropriate point of entry.

(Figure 10-2 Firefighters should avoid crawling over heavy content. When necessary, crawl over material and then use pathways. In this picture a FDNY firefighter is crawling over the clutter found inside a Brooklyn Garage. Photo credit Lloyd Mitchell)

Firefighters who encounter a large pile or stack of debris when making entry should crawl over the stacks as a last resort (Figure 10-1). Not knowing what is in the pile of belongings is too big of a risk, as the contents could collapse, trapping the firefighter. Climbing up and over can also cause a firefighter's PPE to ride up, exposing skin to the super-heated environment. One of the most at-risk areas is the firefighter's pants legs. There have been documented cases of firefighters burning their legs when coming into contact with smoldering debris when pant legs expose skin (Writers, 2015).

Entry

Constant situational awareness and TIC use is essential for firefighters making an interior attack in heavy content conditions. Using the TIC can give firefighters a more informed assessment of the current conditions. Constantly scanning the environment, in shorter intervals than in a non-cluttered environment, should be done due to the shielding effects of the stacks. Extra scanning of the ceiling area is of increased importance, as firefighters could be shielded from the conditions do to the surrounding clutter.

If a TIC is not available, firefighters should rely on good situational awareness with continual use of their senses (Figure 10-2). Monitoring neutral plane height, smoke density, turbulence of the underside of the neutral plane, and fire noise is essential. Compound more than one of these variables, and quick retreat is indicated. The lack of a TIC and high stacks of debris can be a recipe for firefighter disaster and should weigh heavily into the go/no-go assessment (Figure 10-3).

(Figure 10-3 Using the TIC to assess the hottest and coldest parts of the rooms before entry will help firefighters identity flowpaths and pathways. In this picture firefighters learn how to use the TIC During Kill the Flashover 2014, Photo Credit Jeff Harkey)

Using a combination of situational awareness and a TIC will allow the interior crews to constantly analyze the need to continue the push or retreat. For interior crews experiencing deteriorating conditions and rising temperatures would be advisable to err on the side of caution due to the lack of secondary means of egress. With windows and other areas of the building being inaccessible, it is better to retreat and use a more defensive mindset. If the fire were to grow, there would be no escape for the crews other than the point of entry.

Enhanced water

Enhanced Water Streams (EWS) are fire streams where a concentrate has been added to improve the performance of water. According to the official NFPA definition, a wetting agent is, "a concentrate that, when added to water, reduces the surface tension and increases its ability to penetrate and spread". The NFPA definition of a wetting agent solution is, "water to which a wetting agent has been added" (NFPA 18, 2010, p. 18-6). Using enhanced water streams on heavy content fires has many advantages over regular water. Adding concentrate to water cools the environment faster, uses less water, produces less hot steam, and adds knockdown power to attack streams (Oke, S. 2015).

The benefits of EWS during heavy content fires are amplified by the amount of fuel available in addition to lack of access to the fire. Fire departments should begin to research the different types of solutions, delivery methods, and cost well in advance of a heavy content fire. EWS itself is worthy of an entire book explaining selection and application. This chapter will focus on applications for heavy content fires.

Applying hose streams with concentrate added can be accomplished in two ways. First, the concentrate can be flowed at a very low percentage through a non-aerated nozzle where the concentrate is allowed to soak deep into the stacks of belongings and causes the water to cling to the stuff. Utilizing concentrate in this manner goes against the way many firefighters have traditionally been taught about the application of EWS. Many firefighters believe the class A foam concentrates are used to create a foam blanket over the top of the surface to inhibit burning. Applying a foam blanket on the surface is an option, but it is also more difficult application process due to the constricted amount of available spaces after the heavy content has piled up. By choosing concentrate with a lower percentage firefighters can use normal nozzles in a direct to the seat application or an indirect application. The key to applying concentrate at this lower percentage is the complete coverage of the belongings. Soaking down the surface area and allowing the EWS to penetrate deep into the stuff is where the lower percentage has benefits.

Choosing to apply concentrate to create foam blankets is another valid application of EWS. This requires firefighters to use walls and ceilings to bounce fire streams off in order to create a foam blanket. Using products such as high expansion foam can make this process easier, but more expensive. High expansion foam is not readily available in most districts, and exploration of its availability should be sought during the pre-fire planning process. Creating a foam blanket with normal class A foam on top of massive amounts of belongings can also be more complicated due to the varying height of the stacks inside the room. The amounts of foam concentrate needed may outweigh the benefits due to the different heights of belongings, causing the foam blanket to form in an ineffective way.

The preferred method of EWS application is to use lesser concentrations to allow the water to seep deep into the stacks of belongings. Using the EWS streams in this way has the additional benefit of reducing the chances of horizontal fire spread and rapidly changing fire phenomenon such as a flashover. When moisture is absorbed and retained in the stacks of belongings, fire has to dissipate or dehydrate the water in order for the belongings to burn. EWS supports this by keeping the moisture where it is needed.

EWS streams can also be used to paint the walls and the ceilings with a back-and-forth motion. This serves the same purpose as applying it to stacks of debris and can slow horizontal fire spread. The success of this EWS application was recorded in the KTF Burn test 6-2 (Oke, S., 2015). Burn 6-2 compared fire behavior between treated rooms and untreated rooms. EWS was added and the fire was started in order to monitor fire behavior within a pre-treated room. The same test was also carried out in a room where normal un-enhanced water was applied. The results from KTF Burn 6.2 illustrated the benefits of using the EWS to paint the walls and ceiling for favorable fire conditions. Rooms treated with plain water allowed the fire to extend into the attic spaces, whereas the temperatures were lower in EWS treated rooms and in the room of origin, keeping the fire from reaching the attic spaces (Starnes, 2015).

When using EWS streams, close attention must be paid to the runoff. Flows showing signs of EWS runoff need to be re-evaluated. If the concentrate is running, it is not staying on the surface and the benefits will not be seen. Firefighters will need to use patience and keen observation skills when flowing EWS to ensure its proper application.

Smoke blockades

Starting in 2005, German firefighters began to research methods of controlling smoke spread and air flow in structural fires. Different methods, designs, and applications came from this testing. The resulting tool combined a metal frame, a spreader (much like a smoke ejector), and a fiber cloth. Obviously, the fiber cloth had to meet many requirements for both safety and practical reasons (Reick, M., 2012). The cloth chosen had to withstand high heat and create a tight seal around the doorframe. By combining the metal frame, cloth, and spreader, the firefighters were able to control the escaping gases and cold air intake.

Smoke blockades have many different applications in the heavy content environment. The first application is to control the air track for interior firefighters. Using a blockade on entry points gives firefighters more control over the airflow versus closing a door. Many front doors have windows that can fail as temperatures increase, are unable to close around

hose lines, and can become jammed due to large stacks of debris.

(Figure 10-4 Firefighters install a smoke curtain before performing a Vent Enter Search for trapped victims. Photo taken during Project Kill the Flashover 2015 Burn 7-2, Photo

Credit Author)

Each of these variables comes with complications and dangers. Choosing to install the smoke blockade can reduce these variables by making a tighter sealed entryway, allowing for easy escape for firefighters, and allowing space for hose lines.

Installation of the smoke blockade:
- Choose the location
- 3D the door (Apply water to all 3 sides of the door trim)
- Size the curtain
- Install the curtain
- Open the door
- Flowpath Management

Perhaps the biggest variable controlling the size of a fire in a heavy contents building is air flow. Defined by Underwriters Laboratory Firefighter Safety Research as "A Flowpath Management" (FTM), it is a variable that can be controlled. Identifying where the fire's air supply is coming in (intake) and exiting (exhaust) is vital for fire suppression efforts. Once these intake and exhaust points have been identified, firefighters can take efforts to control them.

It may be as simple as closing an exterior door or adding the use of a smoke curtain. Each of these methods can be successful if carried out in a unified approach to air track management.

Firefighters choosing to perform an interior attack should make every effort to control the flowpath before entering. Operating in a bidirectional flow has been proven dangerous even without heavy content conditions. To increase safety, an interior crew should operate in a unidirectional flow with superheated gases going away from advancing firefighters.

A unidirectional flow would direct hot gases away from the advancing crew. An example of this would be entering through a front door, hanging a smoke curtain or closing the door behind the advancing firefighters and opening one exhaust opposite of the entry point. Closing off the air intake behind advancing firefighters will prohibit fresh air from entering the environment and block all exiting superheated gases. Once these gases accumulate at the smoke curtain, the pressure will rise and the flow will change direction towards the exhaust. Heat and smoke work from areas of high pressure to areas of lower pressures, explaining why the heat and smoke will travel towards the exterior of the structure (lower pressure area).

Extreme caution must be used when entering this type of environment in order to eliminate the risk of uncoordinated ventilation. Introducing a new opening in an uncontrolled fashion can cause a very dangerous condition, especially if opened behind an advancing crew. The creation of an additional flowpath can draw fire directly overtop and through firefighters' water streams. Ventilation should be coordinated between interior and exterior firefighters to ensure that all flow paths are accounted for and controlled.

Attacking the Fire:

Direct attack

Many firefighters believe in the characteristics of the solid stream nozzle and apply them to heavy content conditions thinking that the stack of stuff will need a deeper penetration due to the compression of the belongings. While this thought process may have merit when dealing with debris a long distance from the burning room, what is burning and the ability to access the seat of the fire must also be considered. Cluttered conditions reduce the access to the seat of the fire. Without the ability to control the source of burning through direct water application, the conditions can continue to worsen.

An example of this issue was demonstrated during the Project Kill the Flashover (KTF) in 2015. KTF Burn 7-1 was a transitional style attack made with a straight stream water application. The first application was from an exterior window into the room of origin; the second from an interior hallway through the front door as crews advanced toward the room of origin. It was noted that the exterior water application was unable to cool the lower portion of the room containing the point of origin due to the amount of belongings.

After the initial crew left the window to proceed inside the building, the fire quickly returned in size and intensified due to the inability to close the exterior window. KTF Burn 7-1 illustrated the need for air control or a different method of water application, such as indirect attack, due to the limited access to the seat of the fire caused by cluttered conditions (Starnes, 2015).

Applying this knowledge to the use of a straight stream indicates attacking the ceiling while using an indirect attack method. Directing the stream to reflect off the ceiling will allow the water droplets to expand and rain down on top of the burning belongings. It will also begin to cool the environment and keep it from reaching a flashover or rollover state.

Indirectly attacking the fire can disrupt the thermal balance and should be expected when applying water to the super-heated surface of the ceiling (Taylor, J. 2007). If victims are suspected, applying water in this manner may not be indicated due to the disruption of the thermal balance. By keeping themselves below the neutral plane and staying within the pathways, firefighters will reduce the exposure to increased heat.

An indirect attack may be also used from opposing rooms. Using the reach of the nozzle to extend the stream into a room not occupied by the interior firefighters, allows the firefighters a layer of protection from the thermal imbalance. Utilizing the stacks of debris for shielding or remaining at the doorway while attacking the ceiling from outside the involved room allows the reduced airflow to have a smothering affect, assuming no other air tracks are available. This technique is best served by having all windows and doors in place, keeping the resulting steam inside the room to smother the fire out. If a window, door, or roof vent hole is present, the full effects of the stream application may not be realized.

Over-pressure/Under-pressure Attack

Following the test burns completed at the KTF 2015, alternative methods of attack have been identified. One such method of attack is using the European model of Over-pressure/Under-pressure fire attack. This type of fire attack introduces small droplets of water applied to the under pressure side of the fire allowing the air track to pull the moisture provided into the fire room and the seat of the fire. Studies have shown that when used properly this application can be used by interior firefighters while keeping the neutral plane intact.

Advantages of Over-pressure/Under-pressure Application (OUA)

- Using the physics of fire for extinguishment
- Neutral plane stability
- Hot gases are allowed to escape through over-pressure
- Applied from the exterior of building
- Adds moisture to the surface materials

This form of fire suppression is carried out by introducing a narrow fog stream to the base of the neutral plane. Keeping the flow of the nozzle low will keep the size of the water molecules small, thus allowing them to be carried into the intake side of the fire, cooling the seat and allowing any steam or heat to be carried out over the neutral plane. Introducing this fog stream into the base of the neutral plane would be accomplished by spraying water around the 48 inch mark. Once noticeable fire suppression has taken place, crews can adjust their stream pattern and begin an interior push.

Flowing water for short periods will allow for evaluation of the success of the OUA. It may take some time for the molecules of water to travel along the air track to cool the fire and let the gases escape. Constant monitoring of conditions with a TIC and visual cues of steam production should continue throughout the process. Signs of ineffective stream application would include fire growth, no indications of water application, and the neutral plane lowering towards the floor. If one or more of these factors are present, consideration should be made to switch attack methods.

Some variables can reduce the success of the OUA. High stacks of belongings, blocked doorways, and multiple flow paths from uninvolved rooms can influence the success of this style of attack. Reducing the distance between water application and the seat of the fire will increase the chance of success of the OUA.

Dangers of the OUA include:

- Steam production when large droplets are added
- Firefighters being exposed to the byproducts of combustion from the over-pressure side
- Mixing the gases to their Lower Explosive Limits (LEL)

These factors should be taken into consideration when incorporating an OUA. By keeping the water droplets small, the amount of steam will be reduced. Smaller droplets create steam that can be absorbed by the super-heated carbon molecules, limiting the amount of heat inversion (Taylor, J., 2007). Firefighters operating in an OUA attack should stay low and remain out of the exhaust side of the attack. Temperatures of the escaping gases can quickly raise to a level above PPE limits. Using sound tactics of staying low, even when operating outside the building, is the best practice to reduce the level of danger.

Once the water has begun to flow, gases begin to cool and can be taken into the danger zone, entering their LEL. To reduce the likelihood of this occurring, firefighters should continue to cool the environment with short periods of fog application through the under-pressure side. An additional method to reduce this occurrence is the constant application of water to the exterior where the over-pressure side is exiting. Adding moisture to the surface will reduce the chances of gases hitting their LEL by keeping the surface cool enough to stay out of these levels (Taylor, J., 2007).

Hose line Advancing:

Without a doubt, the heavy content environment offers many challenges for an interior hose team. Once the size-up is completed and the risk versus reward decision has been made, it's time to go inside. Choosing the appropriate hose size is essential to the success of the crew. Depending on the fire spread and size, choosing the smaller, more maneuverable hose lines is the best choice. With the clutter slowing the progress of the advancing crews, using the smaller 1 1/2 or 1 3/4 inch attack lines will take some of the workload off the interior crew.

In the clutter, hose teams can encounter challenges such as:
- Stacks of scattered newspapers
- Magazines

- Bottles
- Cans
- Cardboard
- Plastics

(Figure 10-3 Firefighters will encounter many hose line challenges inside heavy content fires. In this photo firefighters deal with these challenges advancing a hose-line. Photo credit Author)

All of the above items will make the push inside challenging. Making sure to stay low and crawl is the recommended means of travel, like in a normal fire, with one difference. Advancing firefighters need to switch from a head down approach to a duck walk style. Keeping the weight balance toward the back leg will allow a firefighter to sound floors, and a small window of opportunity to turn and jump if the floor decking is weakened from extended burn times. Continual sounding of the floor with a tool or the hose stream should help determine if the floor is intact.

When one or more of the above find their way to the floor, it becomes extremely slick for the crews and traction will be difficult. This problem is compounded once the water has been applied. If a firefighter was to try to walk through this slick environment, the fall risk would be too great. Keeping low with weight shifted toward the back while using a wide base can allow the advancement to continue and offer a safer means of advancing.

A firefighter may need to roll over into a sitting position and use his legs to stabilize themselves as they pull the hose. Finding a solid surface, such as a doorframe as a base point, allows the firefighter to use his legs to pull the hose without experiencing the loss of traction. Using the environment can aid in the hose advancement if a firefighter is experiencing a slippery crawl.

Careful attention should be paid to keeping the

stacks in place, if possible. Keep in mind that there can be interior clutter collapse that may be blocking the means of egress, kink hose lines or trap a firefighter within an area. Once the belongings start to collapse, it could trigger a chain reaction and bring down an entire room full of clutter.

Another challenge for interior firefighters is nozzle control while crawling through the treacherous environment. If a firefighter doesn't control the bell on the nozzle during the advancement, it can open discharging water at the wrong time, making the floor slicker.

Keeping the water off the newspapers, magazines, and cardboard will allow for more traction. Even dry materials can be dangerous, but once the water has been applied it becomes exponentially harder to crawl over. Controlling the nozzle will also prevent the inadvertent knocking over of the stacks.

A major concern for the advancing hose team is the shielding that the heavy content environment provides them from the super-heated environment. If the stacks extend above the heads of the crawling firefighters it can shield them from the true temperature inside. If the only part of the firefighter being exposed to the heat is the top of the helmet, it can lead to a false sense of security. Most firefighters use the heat they feel with their ears as a temperature gauge. In the "goat paths", the firefighter may not be feeling the true heat level, especially if the stacks are only a few feet wide. Understanding the insulating effects, firefighters should use the TIC to continually scan interior temperatures.

Hose Team Challenges

Narrowed pathways, piles of debris, and other results of heavy content will slow the progress of the interior crews and increase their workload, while also decreasing the amount of air time they have to work inside. Firefighters should take these challenges into consideration when entering a cluttered environment. Increasing crew sizes can distribute the workload between multiple firefighters and reduce the risk interior crews will face

Following the identification of the heavy content environment, firefighters should evaluate crew sizes before entering. Using the common two firefighter approach can lead to dangerous situations as the backup firefighter, often the officer, will be separated from the nozzle firefighter dealing with the pathways and clutter. Staying within the pathways, the officer will have to manage pinch points while nozzle firefighters continue the push. With the officer unable to evaluate the conditions, being separated from the nozzle, firefighters must be aware of their surroundings

To combat this issue the crew will need to make some adjustments. The first option is to place the fire officer on the nozzle. This goes against many firefighters' "best practices" for normal fires, but heavy content fires are NOT normal fires. Placing the officer on the nozzle will allow them to stay aware of the entire situation and constantly monitor conditions. It will also allow them to continually evaluate the risk versus reward. High heat, low visibility, and no visible fire will direct the retreat of the interior crew, the active cooling of the environment, or both.

Adding additional firefighters to the interior crew is the best option. Increasing the crew size from the standard two firefighters to three or even four firefighters allows the officer to stay with nozzle while the two backup firefighters manage pinch points and clear debris that may fall on the advancing hose line. Today's limited staffing situations in many departments may be a determining factor whether an interior attack can or cannot be initiated. The limited staff of the first arriving crew may choose an alternative means of fire control while waiting for additional resources needed to progress into the structure.

When firefighters are operating inside a cluttered environment, additional attention should be directed towards air consumption rates. The increased work volume presented by the clutter will lessen the amount of work time available inside.

It is essential for firefighters to monitor their air supply and the officer to monitor the air supply of all of the firefighters. Work times should be shortened due to the likelihood of falling clutter caused by advancing firefighters.

(Firefighters should not push forward if they become caught by wires as it may tighten the up. In this picture firefighter recruits from Worth County mitigate the box of frustration. Photo Credit Hope Baidwin *Photography Tifton GA)*

Beginning the exit with greater available air supply will offer firefighters an extra layer of safety in case their retreat pathway has become compromised.

Depending on what is being stored in the collection, firefighters may encounter additional hazards. One of the most concerning hazards is the potential for entanglement in the debris. Anything from multiple extension cords, yarn collections, Christmas lights, or similar hazards may be found. It is essential for firefighters entering a cluttered environment to have a good understanding in practical applications of dealing with these entanglement hazards.

Some common techniques in dealing with these situations include:

Swim technique: Firefighters can use their arms in a swimming motion to capture any entanglements that have hooked on to their Self Contained Breathing Apparatus (SCBA). It is essential for firefighters to resist the urge to push forward, as this will tighten the entanglement. Once resistance is felt, the firefighter should stop forward progression and use his arms in an overhead swinging action, like freestyle swimming, to locate the entanglement. Once located, the firefighter should retreat to loosen the entanglement and continue the swimming motion until the entanglement has been cleared (McCormack, & Pressler, 1998).

Pass through: Using a pass through technique is the preferred method of navigating the pathways. It can require firefighters to use a reduced profile by loosening their SCBA straps and pulling their cylinder underneath one of their arms.

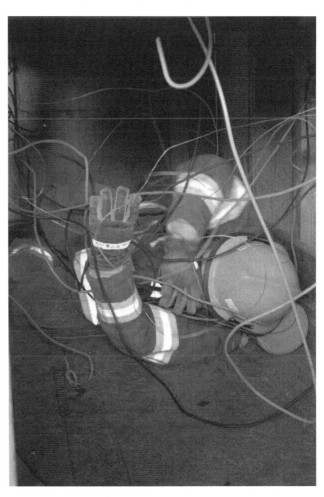

(Figure 10-7 Firefighters can use the path through method for dealing with entanglements. In this picture recruit firefighters from Worth County deal with the box of frustrations. Photo Credit Hope Baidwin Photography)

Understanding the challenges presented when using this type of entanglement mitigation is essential, as many firefighters experience complications with returning the SCBA to their backs (McCormack, & Pressler, 1998). If the pathway requires this type of mitigation during the initial fire attack, serious risk versus reward analysis should be completed.

Nozzle sweep: Using the hose stream to sweep the floor and clear a path is a technique that can be applied if the hoarding is at a lower level. Level 1-3 will be below waist level and can be cleared with the power of the hose stream. If this technique is chosen, the heat and conditions of the room and the potential for thermal disruption must be considered.

Hook and pull: Using a tool to grab the stacks of stuff and pull them over to flatten out the stacks is a labor intensive option. Pulling stacks of stuff over will require more work, time, and reduce air time. The potential for unstable stacks is present when combining contents of the tumbled debris. It also can raise the level that the firefighter is crawling by 1 to 2 feet, exposing them to a higher heat level.

Knock over the piles: The final option is for a firefighter to bulldoze his way in. Lowering a shoulder to make the push inside while pushing the piles over is the least preferred method. It has the most potential for collapse, entrapment, and thermal dangers for the interior crew. Knocking over the piles of debris also increases the likelihood of covering an unannounced victim. Taking the time to level stacks of debris is the most labor-intensive method dealing with the clutter. Due to the labor intensive action combined with the possibility of covering unannounced victims, it should be reserved as a last option.

Each one of the above techniques is a viable option for dealing with extreme cluttered conditions. They can be used individually, be combined, or deployed at any time during an interior fire operation. When considering what type of technique to deploy, firefighters should consider the potential for unannounced victims. If there is reported entrapment or unaccounted occupants, the stacks should be kept in place.

CHAPTER 11:
DEFENSIVE OPERATIONS

Many heavy content fires will present an unacceptable risk for interior fire operations, leaving firefighters to battle the fire from the exterior of the building. Defensive operations does not eliminate the dangers, rather it offers a new set of complications. First and foremost is the danger of collapse due to an overloaded structure in disrepair.

Collapse zone recognition should be the primary consideration when choosing a defensive posture. A heavy content building can be under a large amount of stress before the first gallon of water is applied. Firefighters should establish a 1 1/2 height distance away from the building as the collapse zone and set up their operations outside this zone. Positioning apparatus at the corners of the building offers the most protection from collapse. If the walls were to fall, they would do so away from the apparatus.

Depending on the amount of yard clutter, apparatus placement can be a challenge. Privacy fences, chain link fences, and stacks of debris around the exterior all complicate this process. When deciding on apparatus placement, aerial apparatus should be considered first. Working around the aerial apparatus with engine placement to support its operation will allow the use of master streams, access overtop the debris, and will also allow for an aerial view of the property.

An additional concern when placing apparatus is the potential for horizontal fire spread on the exterior debris. Fires that progress into the exposed materials surrounding the building could gain strength with wind and rapidly surround parked fire apparatus. This situation was experienced by the Kentland Volunteer Fire Department on a third alarm warehouse yard fire. Kentland's Rescue Engine 33 was parked more than 300 feet from the original seat of the fire when the wind shifted and directed the fire into stacks of Styrofoam, engulfing the pumper and severely burning it (Kelleher, T 2015).

Utilizing the pre-fire planning process gives firefighters the opportunity to discuss apparatus placement well in advance of the fire. As noted in a prior chapter, cluttered homes can now be identified using Google Earth's overhead view to allow for strategic planning of apparatus well in advance of the fire.

Factors indicating an initial choice of defensive posture include:
- Limited staffing
- Poor access
- Limited water supply
- Confirmation of all occupants out
- Heavy fire volume
- Unsafe points of entry
- No secondary means of egress
- Imminent collapse
- No-go assessment following 380° size-up

Any one of the above factors would indicate a defensive posture. This approach can begin with outside attack and then transition to an interior attack if conditions improve.

One of the key elements in fighting a heavy content fire is using the compressed spaces to help extinguish the fire. Limiting the available air while cooling from the safest location can be effective. The methods used to carry out this task may include some non-traditional ways of attacking the fire.

Tools such as piercing nozzles, cellar nozzles, fog nails, smoke curtains, and positive pressure fans with water flowing through them are some of the examples of non-traditional ways of battling heavy content fires in defensive mode.

Starting Point

Applying the 380° size-up to the defensive process can direct the application of the first water streams. Working from the hottest to coldest spots, if possible, will speed the extinguishment process. Similar to the offensive go/no-go assessment, the thermal imaging camera (TIC)-directed attack is essential for decision making. Even if the fire is showing, the TIC scan should be completed as the fire showing is where it is at now and the TIC can indicate where it is going. Killing active flaming while understanding and controlling the air track in coordination makes the attack most efficient.

During the 380° size-up and decision making process, firefighters should be on guard for flaming that is nearing any exterior clutter. Adding moisture or wetting down the exterior clutter can reduce the likelihood of horizontal fire spread. Utilizing fog streams with EWS for this application will keep the stacks of debris in place while adding the smaller droplets that can soak deeper into the stacks. Keeping this moisture in place can reduce the chance of fire spread, so firefighters should keep the exterior clutter wet while fighting the fire.

Kill Active Flaming

Discovering and attacking any visible flame is first priority once the size-up is complete. Directing first fire streams into these areas as quickly as possible will result in less fire spread and reduce the chances of gas ignition. When determining the location for fire streams, firefighters should take into consideration the challenges of maneuvering around the exterior clutter. If access is blocked or restricted due to this clutter, firefighters will need to use the reach of the streams to kill the active flaming.

If access is limited, this may indicate the need for a larger caliber stream with a longer reach. An example of this would be attacking the side C of a building with an extensive amount of clutter in the back yard protected by high privacy fences. Once the fence is removed, the clutter may prohibit firefighters from gaining access to the fire room.

Understanding the challenges, firefighters may choose a 2 1/2 inch hose line, versus a smaller 1 3/4 inch hand line, that will offer greater stream reach to compensate for this challenge. Choosing a larger caliber line will require additional resources for deployment, which may factor into the choice of line size. Having pre-rigged master streams such as the Akron Mercury Nozzle or Task Force Tips' Blitzfire nozzle set up for single firefighter deployment will aid in this process.

If exterior clutter is extreme, deploying the master stream of an aerial device or the deck gun of an engine may be the first choice. Establishing water supply quickly will aid in the deployment of these two master streams. While first priority should typically be to contain the fire to the building of origin, fire conditions may dictate the need for exposure control as a first priority. Once exposures are not a concern, master streams should be directed into the active flaming.

A major concern with deploying master streams flowing thousands of gallons per minute (GPM) is the additional weight being added to the structure. Water weighs in at 8.33 pounds per gallon, and the additional weight delivered to the contents of the building could begin the collapse process.

Utilizing master streams as a last resort can offer an extended amount of working time in the collapse zone if fire conditions dictate. Choosing two smaller sized lines versus one larger sized line could offer increased mobility and the required GPMs if the hose teams work in unison.

Piercing Attack

Keeping all windows and doors in place to limit available air can help contain the fire from spreading. Choosing a through-the-wall attack with a piercing nozzle or opening small holes for nozzle placement is a viable option when dealing with a heavy content environment. A basic understanding of how stuff is stored inside the building is essential for applying these tactics. Piercing the side of the building into a stack of belongings will result in minimal, if any, fire suppression success.

Piercing nozzles should be introduced high on the exterior wall to ensure that it is overtop the stacks of belongings. This may require firefighters to use small ladders to climb over exterior debris or to have enough reach to make the access point available. Keeping the window in place when applying the piercing attack will enhance the cooling effects of the water stream while limiting fire growth.

(Figure 11-1 Firefighters can use a piercing attack to increase safety. Photo Jeff Harkey)

During Project Kill the Flashover (KTF) 2015, Battalion Chief Lars Agerstrand of the Värnamo Fire and Rescue Service in Sweden introduced the attendees to a nozzle used in the European fire service. The fog nail is a small piercing nozzle that can be applied from the exterior through holes created with either a drill or by hammering the fog nail through the wall. Using fine mists and a wide-angle fog, the fog nail delivers small droplets of water that are used to cool the environment and add moisture to the contents.

During the KTF, Burn 7-3 firefighters utilized the fog nail in combination with enhanced water. Success of this delivery model was evident during the burn down process of the home. The fog nail was flowed during the initial fire attack process. Thermal imaging video from the interior showed its effectiveness, even with the interior door open and an air track available.

Once the decision was made to begin the burn down process of the test home, the fire was allowed to consume the building. In reviewing the burn down process video, noticeable differences were noted between rooms treated with the fog nail and EWS versus the non-treated. As the fire continued to grow, the room that was treated with a fog nail was the last to burn. The KTF Burn 7-3 was a great example of how the use of this European nozzle can be applied in the American fire service.

Until the fog nail becomes available to the American fire service, firefighters can substitute a traditional piercing nozzle. Applying the American style piercing nozzle into a room can be accomplished by creating the hole and then placing the piercing nozzle, or by using one firefighter to hold the nozzle while the other hammers through the exterior of the home. The two firefighter method may be complicated by exterior stacks of belongings and the inability to place two ladders side by side.

Conditions may dictate that the piercing nozzle be applied through the upper pane of a window or through the window frame itself. Every effort should be taken to keep the window in place in order to limit air intake. Once the piercing nozzle has been placed, short bursts from the nozzle should be the initial attack method to also allow assessment for the effectiveness of the piercing.

Introducing a water stream such as the piercing nozzle should be restricted to when there is confirmation of no victims trapped, as the amount of steam created by these small droplets of water may decrease the survivability for any trapped victims. Caution should be taken when using this application, as the window may be compromised when the water begins to flow.

If the piercing nozzle is not available, a standard fog nozzle can be deployed in its place. Creating a small hole and introducing the tip on the 30° fog or wider can accomplish the same attack. It should also be applied high on the exterior wall above the stacks of debris on the inside. Just like the piercing nozzle attack, short bursts should be used initially to allow for assessment of its effectiveness.

Another choice for nozzles in heavy content fires is the Bresnan Distributor Nozzle, otherwise known as a cellar nozzle. The Shepherdstown, West Virginia Fire Department illustrated its use during a two alarm heavy content fire. The Shepherdstown firefighters attached the Bresnan Distributor Nozzle to a 2 1/2 inch attack line on the end of an attic ladder. Using hose straps to secure the nozzle, they slid the attic ladder into the available spaces above the stacks of belongings. The opening required to do this procedure would be larger than that of the piercing nozzle.

It is essential for firefighters to understand that the opening could create an air track as they begin to open up and place this nozzle in-service. Limiting the size of the opening will increase the effectiveness of the hose stream.

The use of these piercing-style attacks can also be applied to attic fires with suspected and known heavy content environments. If the fire has extended into the attic, the same complications should be expected there. Attic spaces are often used as initial storage for compulsive hoarders as it does not affect day-to-day living. These spaces can become as full, if not fuller, than the usable spaces downstairs.

When suspecting that an attic is full, firefighters can attack it from the top using any of the nozzles and applications referenced above. While there is no commonality in levels of hoarding found in attic spaces, firefighters should assume that the space is near its capacity when attacking fire.

If aerial apparatus are available, the same top-down approach can be used with master streams. Just as with the side attack, all efforts should be made to limit air intake while making the stream application more effective. As previously mentioned, the use of master streams will deliver more weight into the structure than that of normal sized hose lines. Using the short burst process with aerial master streams will allow the assessment of how much water will be needed to control the fire.

The Need to Open Up

Following the initial knockdown and fire control, the building will need to be opened up to finish the extinguishment process. This process should begin with the room of origin and work from the original hottest areas to the coldest areas to ensure fire control. All steps in the process of opening the structure should be completed in a coordinated fashion, either directed by the interior firefighters or with no firefighters inside the structure. Creating openings in the side of the building will create air tracts and the dangers associated with both.

After choosing the location to begin the open-up process, firefighters should use the windowsill removal method to gain access to the room. Removing the window, using a saw to cut down the support plate on both sides, and then removing the base of the window will allow for a larger opening for belongings to be removed. Choosing the appropriate saw for this task is essential.

Debris inside the house may prohibit the use of a long blade, which may not be successful removed. A rotary saw with an all-purpose chopper style blade is the best choice when dealing with windowsill removals. A rotary saw does not go as deep as a chainsaw, and the chopper blade will be able to handle any metal wires or nails encountered during this procedure. Firefighters should ensure the electricity has been disconnected to reduce the risk of electric shock.

(Figure Using aerial apparatus can aid in extinguishment and in the opening up process. In this picture FDNY ladder 113 is used for ventilation and fire attack. Photo Credits Lloyd Mitchell.)

Removing the glass should begin to allow hot gases to escape. Firefighters should not stand in front of a window when it is removed. Escaping gases, once mixed with air, can reach their flammable limits, causing rollover, flashover, or backdraft. To reduce the likelihood of this happening, water should be applied to all three sides of the frame. Once the gases have escaped and the windowsill has been removed, firefighters can use pike poles and/or roof hooks to begin pulling the debris out of the building.

Pulling the debris outside the window can open up the room for entry, allow firefighters to assess any structural damage, and provide access for further water application. Having direct access into the room provides a safer environment for firefighters to work in, as the debris will need to be removed for complete extinguishment and to reduce the likelihood of re-kindle.

Firefighters should be on the lookout for bulging walls, sagging roofs, and an extensive burn of support members. If one or more of these conditions are noted, firefighters should be removed from the building and the findings communicated to the Incident Commander.

Demolishing the Building

(Figure Heavy Content Conditions may require the use of a bulldozer to aid in suppression. In this picture the Delaware County PA firefighters use a Cat to completely extinguish this middle of the row heavy content fire. Photo credits Delaware County PA)

One of the most common types of defensive operations is to demolish the building. Once all efforts have been implemented, or the structure becomes too unstable, the best choice may be to tear the building down. While it seems like a simple procedure that has frequently been used in the past, it can be complicated to achieve during an active fire. Using an excavator while a fire is ongoing requires the coordinated effort of firefighters, equipment operators, and Incident Commanders to ensure safe operations as the building is demolished.

One of the biggest challenges when demolishing a building is the need to protect the equipment operator. As the building comes down, pockets of smoke, fire, or both can be released, exposing the operator to the dangers associated with it. Protecting the operator's respiratory system is critical.

Training operators in the use of SCBA should occur prior to the need to use it. Fire departments should add this training to their normally scheduled operations. Identifying available demolition companies, saving their contact information, and learning about their operators ahead of time is a great asset when such a company is needed. In the volunteer arena, the best case scenario would be an operator that is also a firefighter.

If no firefighter-operators are available, a training session should be set up with local demolition companies to explain how to coordinate the efforts to demolish and extinguish. This training should occur annually, as many companies change operators during a one year period.

While identifying these companies, a fire department should confirm that each company is available on a 24/7 basis. If a fire happens at 02:30 on Christmas night, will they be available? If not, the department may need to find another company to call on. Availability may already be known and documented in a jurisdiction's Emergency Management Plan.

One of the challenges faced when using machinery to tear down a building is the recovery of people trapped inside. Many cases have shown this is a real danger. When a fire becomes too big or too dangerous, an Incident Commander must make the decision to switch into a recovery mode. Once this decision has been made and the excavation has begun, the use of spotters and an organized search pattern should be used. The skill of the operator will be tested as he uses the equipment to remove the structure bit by bit and piece by piece, all while searching for the lost victim. Establishing a system of hand signals, commands, and directions before a fire happens allows the best chance to recover a trapped occupant. There are many dangers associated with working around hydraulic equipment, including crushing injuries from rotating booms, collapsing debris, and blown hydraulic lines.

The use of an aerial master stream with the

excavation is a great combination. Using the elevated stream as a water curtain can keep the smoke level pushed down and keep firefighters at a safe distance from the swinging arm.

During the operation, a dedicated Rapid Intervention Team (RIT) should be assigned for the equipment operator. The demolition process can expose the operator to numerous dangers, and the RIT team should be trained and equipped to respond if needed. Additional equipment that may be needed includes stabilization struts or cribbing to shore up the building or the excavator if needed.

Choosing to stay exterior to fight a heavy content fire is the safest approach. Firefighters should not risk lives to battle a blaze in hoarding conditions once all victims are accounted for. Utilizing non-traditional approaches to battling the flames can provide a safer environment. At any time, if conditions change or viable victims have been announced, operational modes can be changed from offensive to defensive and back to offensive. Fire scenes are dynamic, and constant evaluation of attack strategies should continue throughout the incident.

CHAPTER 12:
SEARCHING FOR OCCUPANTS

Without a doubt, the number one priority of all first responders is to save lives. From a working structural fire to a medical emergency, the ability to find trapped occupants is an essential skill that should be practiced constantly. When hoarding conditions are added to the equation, many victims can go overlooked or not be found at all. Searching for victims inside massive amounts of clutter can push the most experienced firefighters to their limits.

The words that no firefighter wants to hear are "victims trapped." Those words send hearts racing as minds are focused on the task at hand. When the words, "You are responding to a heavy content environment," are added, responding personnel must understand the differences between the heavy content environment and the typical environment that have been detailed in earlier chapters. From the non-typical points of entry to the sheer amount of belongings, the challenges will be numerous.

Firefighters facing the task of locating and removing a victim in a heavy content environment have to decide how to make the most positive improvement for the victim in the shortest amount of time. Doing so may indicate the need for fire suppression before searching for the victim. If staffing is limited, this decision becomes more complex. Short-staffed crews need to be more efficient in their operation. A search crew entering a cluttered area may be slowed by the contents, allowing more time for fire growth and spread if uncontrolled. Choosing the best option for fire control while making every effort to begin the search process is essential, and should be based on sound decision-making.

Locating the Victim

Determining the last known location of the victim will both direct and speed up the search for trapped occupants. Many searches begin after a well investigated size-up that includes the number of cars in the driveway, time of day, and interviews with witnesses that may have knowledge of the victim's location.

One variable not present in "normal" living conditions is the inability of an occupant to sleep in the bedroom or utilize the living room for recreation. As their collection grows, occupants may sleep in other parts of their homes once their bedrooms are unlivable. Firefighters should take this variable into consideration when planning a search.

There is no consistency in what rooms become cluttered first, as this varies from person to person. It can vary as much as the content someone chooses to collect. One variable that remains constant is the filling of the attic and basement first. It makes perfect sense to expect these rooms to be the first ones filled, as most homeowners use these spaces to store their seasonal belongings such as Christmas decorations.

While there is no clinical data to support this theory, it should be assumed that these two spaces will be overloaded with belongings.

Once the basement and attic spaces are filled, the occupant will begin to fill any empty container that will hold possessions. The collection might begin in the bedroom, causing the occupant to sleep in another room. Unlivable bedrooms can make a vent-enter-search procedure ineffective if the occupant has filled the bedrooms, and could cost the occupant precious time and the firefighters their lives if they make the incorrect choice.

One common finding, although not supported by clinical data, is that the last two rooms that will be filled are bathrooms and kitchens. Taking this into consideration when deciding to conduct a search offers valuable points of reference. If these rooms are often the last to be filled, they can also be the last point of escape to which trapped occupants retreat in the event of a fire.

Making the Determination

To determine the last known position of the victims and the point of entry to be used in the search, an all-inclusive approach to where, when, how, and if a search will be performed should be used.

These variables to determine an occupant's location should be added to the normal size-up process:
- Neighbors' input
- Family members' input
- Primary point of entry
- Size of pathways
- Choosing Orientation

- Wall Searching

Many firefighters are taught from day one to search for victims by remaining in contact with an exterior wall while searching. Right and left handed search patterns have long been the gold standard for searching. In the heavy content environment, this means of orientation can be dangerous. If a firefighter is to try keeping his hand attached to an exterior wall, he could easily be distracted by the stacks of stuff and find himself in the middle of a room, disoriented and lost.

While left and right handed search patterns can be used in the hoarded environments, they should be used vary rarely and with extreme caution.

Oriented Search

An oriented search is a type of search pattern where one firefighter remains in the doorway, keeping his orientation, while a second, and sometimes third, firefighter searches the interior spaces, keeping in constant voice contact. Using flashlights, voice contact, or a short section of rope allows the searching firefighter to keep in communication with the oriented firefighter. This technique is a faster and more efficient way to perform a rapid search for victims in a heavy content environment. It also makes for a safer environment for the firefighter conducting the search.

In a cluttered area, an oriented search can be complicated, with stacks of belongings slowing the searching firefighter's progress or reducing the volume of communication between the firefighters. It also limits the use of a rope to keep in contact with the oriented firefighter.

Thermal Image Orientation Search

Since the invention of the thermal imaging camera (TIC), the searching process has become quicker and more direct. Being able to see through the smoke allows searching firefighters the ability to make a direct path to where the victim is located. It also allows the directing firefighter the ability to keep oriented to their location inside the structure. However, firefighters should not depend solely on the TIC for orientation, as it could fail, leaving the firefighters disoriented to their location inside the building. By making the searching process more efficient, this allows the victim a greater chance for survival.

A best practice for TIC searches is to use one firefighter to direct a second in search patterns while they remain oriented to position. Much like the oriented search, this will allow the firefighter to keep a constant orientation. Scanning the room with the TIC, firefighters should look for fire conditions and be watching for cold spaces. These cold areas are where the victim would have the best chance of survival due to temperature and stored air. Many modern TIC cameras have the ability to track the coldest part of the room. Looking for these cooler spaces can also identify pathways used by the occupants. Searching firefighters should use these pathways to search for the victim, as they often are found in the pathways.

When scanning for victims with the TIC, firefighters should be aware of the potential for victims to be covered in debris. It is common for victims trying to escape a fire to be overcome by smoke and then fall to the floor. When this occurs, there is a potential for debris to cover the victim. When scanning with the TIC, firefighters should look for hands, feet, faces, and stacks that appear to be disturbed from their normal storage presentation. An example would be a stack of belongings in the middle of a well-established pathway. If fallen debris is found, firefighters should pay close attention and complete a quick sort of the debris to ensure no victims are present.

As mentioned above, firefighters who do not use sound firefighting practices and rely solely on the TIC could find themselves in a lost, disoriented situation if the batteries or camera were to fail. Keeping constant awareness to location is essential. Each brand of TIC camera offers different modes of operation. Firefighters must take the time to learn their TIC well in advance of entering a heavy content environment.

Rope Search

Choosing to search for a victim while remaining in contact with the outside by using a search rope can be a great way to remain oriented. Many fire departments choose this method and carry various types of set ups, from rope bags to plastic containers with rope. Some of the complications of using this type of search in a heavy content environment are the risk of collapsing belongings, exposing the rope to smoldering debris, and multiple entanglement hazards.

By far, the biggest danger of using a search rope is the risk of smoldering debris burning through the rope. As searching firefighters advance through the stacks of belongings, the rope can come into contact with surfaces that are hot enough to burn through the rope. If a fire department uses a rope that is NOT high heat rated, a search team could find themselves lost in the mountains of debris.

Fire departments should choose high temperature rated search ropes, which are commercially available from various manufacturers. One example is the RIT 900 rope from Sterling Rope, which is rated to 932°F. This rope is more expensive to purchase but offers a greater level of safety for firefighters.

Many fire departments cannot afford the more expensive search rope. In this case, a good practice is to utilize an uncharged, double-jacketed fire hose. All departments carry it, it's portable, lightweight, and in the event of a rapid fire progression it can be charged to help shield firefighters. The downside of carrying an uncharged hose line is the dragging process. Search ropes are carried in an over-the-shoulder bag and deployed from it, while uncharged hose lines will be advanced with the bulk of the hose being on the exterior of the structure, slowing the search progress.

The hose line's double jacket will help prevent it from melting and burning through. While it may not be as practical as a rope bag, it is a better option than using a nylon rope that can melt when exposed to the smoldering debris.

Vent-Enter-Search

One solid option for victim search and removal is the process of identifying a location, accessing it through a window, quickly searching, and removing the victim. Vent, Enter, Search (VES) is a tactic that has been used by firefighters worldwide for years. Applying this tactic to the heavy content environment is acceptable with some additional factors and adjustments:

Vent: Clear the window.

Enter: Crawl through the window below the escaping hot gases.

Search: Shut the interior door to isolate the room and then search the room.

Firefighters using VES should expect that the interior door will not close due to the clutter. Being unable to close this interior door can create an air track when the window is removed. If the interior door cannot be closed, the creation of a lower pressure area can draw heat, smoke, and flames into the room, making conditions worse for firefighters and occupants.

Before window removal, firefighters should remove a small pane or slightly open the window to investigate whether the interior door can be closed. Using the TIC to scan the stacks is the best option to aid in this assessment. Firefighters should open the window on the low or under-pressure side to limit gases from mixing with the available air, thereby keeping them out of the flammable range.

If the door cannot be closed, a secondary means of air control should be used. Placing a smoke blockade or creating a small opening at the top of the window for gas escape while opening the bottom for entry can limit the air track. If a smoke curtain is not available, water should be applied to the exterior of the window to cool gases that are escaping through the opening to help keep them from reaching their Lower Flammable Limits.

Another available option in a VES operation with an interior door that cannot be closed is to cool the environment. Gas cooling with short pulses of water from a fog nozzle set at 30° can help cool the gases while keeping the neutral plane in place. Using this method may require three firefighters instead of the traditional two. One to search, one to watch over the search with the TIC, and the third to gas cool during the process.

Upon entering the window, firefighters should locate

the pathway quickly. Getting low towards the floor is essential both for firefighters' safety and victim location. If no pathway is found, firefighters should consider the room is being used for storage space and not a living space. TIC scanning can be used to identify the colder spots of the room and to identify the presence of a pathway.

Combination Approach

When facing a heavy content condition requiring a search to find and remove victims, firefighters should choose a combination of all of the above orientation types to ensure their safety. Combining search ropes, TIC use, and an oriented search will give firefighters the best probability of search success.

Although the combination of tactics can slow the searching firefighters, it allows for a constant orientation and a means to escape if the fire conditions deteriorate. It also helps in the management of the belongings that can cover the exit path.

In a search, the first firefighter is the searching firefighter and the second firefighter, who is "directing" the search, is the navigation firefighter. Navigation firefighters should stay observant of the conditions and direct the searching firefighter towards the pockets of space where the victims may be found. The pace will be slower than usual as both firefighters navigate through the pathways.

Searching firefighters should NOT go up and over piles of debris if at all possible. These piles contain unknown types of belongings that may not support the weight of a firefighter in full PPE and SCBA, and could easily cause a firefighter emergency.

Occupants do not crawl over the belongings. They use pathways to travel between rooms. Using these pathways can lead to the only livable spaces, and directly to the victim. This is why pathways should always be used in a hoarding environment. Pathways can also insulate firefighters from the heat as the stacks of stuff can keep some of the radiant heat off of the firefighter by insulating the sides of the pathways. There have been documented cases of hoarding where victims have survived inside burning buildings because they were insulated from the radiant heat due to the massive amounts of belongings.

Victim Removal

Upon locating the victim, removal can offer more challenges as firefighters work to extricate said victim. First and foremost, each firefighter's air supply must be evaluated. Determining which crew member's air supply is the lowest should be the first task after the victim has been found. Once established, this information should be transmitted to the OIC. If the firefighters are low on air, they should begin their exit.

Many fire departments use 20% as the minimum amount of remaining air supply before the crew must exit. This rule should be expanded when operating inside a hoarding environment, as 20% may not be sufficient to give firefighters enough air to make their exit, especially if some of the belongings have collapsed into the pathways.

If something is blocking the pathways, it will require more work to clear and/or lift the victim up and over, thus consuming more air. Firefighters should err on the side of caution to allow an additional safety buffer in case they encounter a blocked means of egress.

After determining firefighters' air supply, searching firefighters should begin to search for means of removal. The navigation firefighter should hand over the rope bag and begin to search for a closer escape route. The reasoning for this practice is the likelihood that the navigation firefighters have more remaining air due to a lower workload than that of the searching firefighter. Roles can be adjusted in this situation depending on actual air volumes found. Blocked windows, doors, and stairways can eliminate possible choices of removal to the point of entry where the search began. Possible secondary points of exit should also be noted as the original search is progressing.

Once the firefighter fans out to start the search for secondary means of egress, communication with the exterior should increase.

"Search Team 1 to command. We are ready for removal. Our location is on the _____ side. Do you have any secondary means of egress?" This communication is vital, as the exterior crew can be taking a proactive approach to the removal. Exterior crews can identify windows, doors, and other pre-made means to egress, or can begin a wall removal to provide direct access to the victim.

Once the point of exit has been established and the removal has begun, crew communication is vital. Pre-determined procedures for victim removal should be understood and used by all crew members. The ready-drag commands reduce confusion, coordinate the firefighters, and make the team more efficient. Sharing the workload between both firefighters will make the rescue faster and lessen the chances that one of the firefighters will have a Mayday.

Keeping the victim inside the pathway will limit the exposure to hot and toxic gases. Using the pathways requires one firefighter at the victim's head and one in the crotch area while removing the victim in a head-first drag. Keeping the profile in line will reduce the chances of debris collapsing and striking the firefighter or victim. To reduce these risks, all firefighters should use both arms and legs in a crawling type profile. Spreading the force over the entire body can help reduce the slipping. Using a handcuff knot around the victim's arms will also reduce the chances of the arms becoming entangled in the belongings.

If a victim must be lifted up and over stacks of stuff, firefighters should stand side by side with the victim if possible. Using the body's natural flexibility allows the firefighters to move the victim over the stacks more safely and quickly. This can be accomplished by lifting the patient while face down, legs first. Using a three part lift can make it easier to go up and over the debris. Firefighters should also pay attention to the patient's head and neck area while maneuvering over the piles.

A major concern for victims that must be taken up and over piles of belongings is the possibility they will receive burns from the contents. Smoldering debris found on the surface of the stacks can cause severe burns to unprotected occupants. Scanning the stacks with a TIC can give removal firefighters a better understanding of where the hottest parts are and allow them to either cool the space or push the smoldering debris out of the way if time permits. If firefighters encounter an increasingly hostile environment, a hasty lift and pull will be needed to limit the amount of time victims are exposed to the hot surfaces.

Firefighters lifting victims up and over the stack to access an exterior window can use an attic ladder to help limit the exposure to burning debris. Using the ladder as a fulcrum on top of the piles can also aid in lifting. Placing the butt end of the ladder inside the window, if possible, will allow exterior firefighters to aid in the rescue.

Sheer brute determination is needed to remove a victim from hoarding conditions. A well placed plan of action that is practiced repeatedly before the alarm happens is essential. This plan begins at the fire station, where crews should incorporate some difficult situations when training on search and removal of victims. Highlighting areas of improvement during training is much better than when faced with a heavy content environment.

CHAPTER 13:
AIR MANAGEMENT

When a firefighter runs out of air they run out of LIFE. As firefighters have constantly been reminded since their first days on the job, the amount of available air is directly proportional to one's operational time. Knowledge of air supply and the associated length of working time is critical to firefighters. When entering a structure that is on fire, especially when heavy content is a factor, air management is an essential skill. The ability to keep a close watch on air consumption rates and time needed to escape is absolutely necessary.

Many firefighters fall into the trap of waiting until their alarm sounds before starting the exiting process. This can be troubling in a heavy content situation, as the clutter may cause extra difficulty in escaping, thus requiring more air. Firefighters, officers, and commanders need to use a monitoring system to ensure that firefighters will have an adequate air supply to escape at the time they enter the structure. This starts with the individual firefighter and extends all the way to the chief, with each level having a process in place to ensure success.

Firefighter Level

Everything starts at the street level. Street level functions are where the rubber meets the road in the fire service, and for air supply the monitoring process begins here. It starts with a close estimate of how long the firefighter can remain on one air cylinder. Whether the department chooses 30, 45, or 60 minute cylinders, they all have an actual amount of time that a firefighter can remain in a hostile environment. The actual time may be significantly less than the reported time on the cylinder.

Each firefighter has a consumption rate that he or she should be aware of. This consumption rate should be established before the alarm sounds and should be revisited monthly. Many variables come into play when discussing the air consumption rates including:

- Weather
- Fitness level

- Increase or decrease in body weight
- Frequency of training on air
- Fatigue
- Workload
- Stress level

These factors illustrate how a firefighter's air consumption rate can increase or decrease throughout their career. One factor that must persist when dealing with these variables is awareness. The individual firefighters should be aware of how long they can make a cylinder last under different situations. From light workloads to heavy, knowing one's consumption rate can keep a firefighter aware of how hard he is working, the length of time until empty, and when he should start the retreat.

Officer Level

Company officers have the added responsibility of monitoring the air consumption of their crew. During fire-ground operations, firefighters can sometimes develop tunnel vision regarding their specific operations. It is the company officer who is responsible for monitoring the entire operation, including their personnel. When in command of a crew inside an

Immediately Dangers to Life and Health environment, the company officer should keep track of all members' air supplies and understand each firefighter's air consumption rate. Knowing or not knowing each firefighter's individual air consumption rate can determine whether an operation is successful or unsuccessful.

This process begins at the firehouse in the form of company level drills to compare the work time of their crew. Setting up drills where all members of a crew can work together in similar conditions can help a company officer determine how each member's air consumption rate is in comparison to each other.

This task can be easy for some smaller departments and nearly impossible for large departments, as they may only work with each other one time a month. To compensate for not knowing the firefighters' air consumption rate, the company officer should ask for updates on their remaining air at varying intervals during the operation. An example is: "Capt. to Firefighter, what is your remaining air supply?" "1200 lbs., Capt." Establishing these intervals at the chiefs level will eliminate the need for a company officer to figure out when to check. Using a benchmarking system takes this responsibility away from the company officer level, as the commander or dispatchers will call out at pre-determined intervals, cueing the officer to inquire about the air level remaining.

At these set intervals the company officer, and even the Incident Commander, will hear the cue and ask for air levels. After receiving them, they will report the lowest member's levels to the Incident Commander. Having constant contact between front line officers and commanders allows decisions to be made with a higher level of certainty. If the interior crew is not making progress by these set intervals, the commander can advise them to retreat or allow them to progress deeper into the fight. Continuous communication between the exterior and interior is needed throughout a response in a hoarding environment. From initial knockdown to the extended overhaul process, communication should remain constant, consistent, and accurate.

Incident Command Level

Commanding an incident is the most demanding job on the fire-ground. Standing outside the building, the commander has a 380° view of the challenges ahead. These challenges include keeping a close watch over the interior crews' air time. Using the same benchmarking system mentioned above in the company officer level section, the commander should be constantly monitoring the amount of time a crew has been inside a hoarded environment.

If the dispatch center does not call out times in a set number of intervals, the commander should keep a close eye on the time or use a stopwatch to allow for a real-time look into elapsed time, not just a perception. In emergency situations time can often seem to be slowed down or sped up in the minds of commanders. Minutes can seem like days, or days can seem like minutes. Either way, the Incident Commander should have an accurate means of telling just how long the crews have been at work.

Using this time frame, the commander can adjust the commands to advance or return, especially during a fire attack. With the compartmentalization of a building's interior caused by the collection of stuff, an interior crew can perceive that they are placing water on the fire when, in reality, they are not getting any knockdown and could be nearing a rapid fire event, such as a flashover. Using actual time will allow the frame of reference to be accurate, detailed, and sound, making sure the interior crews have adequate escape time. One step the Incident Commander can take to help keep track of air consumption time is to assign an aide or Safety Officer to monitor this aspect of the operations.

CHAPTER 14:
OVERHAUL

Once the fire has been placed under control, the dangers from hoarding conditions have not been totally abated, but actually increase. After knockdown has been achieved and operations have switched into the overhaul phase of the incident, the building could be at the biggest risk of collapse. Water weight, fire damage, and shifting debris can all be contributing factors to a localized or complete collapse. At this point in the operation, firefighters can be battling fatigue and have a sense of urgency to finish the job. These factors can contribute to relaxing the attention to signs of danger.

Incident Commanders should also consider calling additional crews to relieve initial firefighters to ensure their safety. Overhauling the large amount of material will continue to increase the workload on firefighters. Using fresh crews for the overhaul process will allow for a more thorough assessment and firefighters who are not wet and exhausted to perform the work.

SCBA Use

A common danger that is often overlooked by firefighters is the need to protect the respiratory system during the overhaul phase of the fire. For years, firefighters have swiftly removed their SCBA following the active phase of firefighting. Overhauling a structure after extinguishment can expose firefighters to the toxic twins (carbon monoxide and hydrogen cyanide) and known carcinogens such as formaldehyde.

The importance of continuing SCBA use until the overhaul is complete should be understood by all firefighters. Adding to the dangers in a heavy content environment is the possibility of uncovering smoldering debris. In the process of moving or removing the belongings for further cooling, firefighters could find pockets of toxic gases released by the smoldering.

Additional respiratory dangers in heavy content environments include the presence of fecal matter, mold, and other biohazards hidden underneath the stacks. During the overhaul process firefighters may uncover one or more of these dangers. Without respiratory protection, firefighters could be exposed to them before discovering their presence.

Hidden pockets of combustion

During the overhaul process, smoke conditions should be monitored. Due to the lack of natural ventilation, heavy content buildings can store more smoke than usual. Smoke is created by unburned fuel that is not currently inside its flammable range or is removed from a heat source.

A hidden danger for firefighters during overhaul is the possibility of the accumulated gases reaching their Lower Explosive Limits and causing a rapid fire phenomenon. Keeping this possibility in mind, firefighters should keep the area wet to reduce the heat and keep the gases out of the flammable ranges. To aid in the overhaul, EWS should continue to be added to assist in the absorption of the moisture.

Pressurizing the area with a positive pressure ventilation (PPV) fan is another option when in the overhaul phase of the fire. Ideally, moisture should be added to the fan's air to keep everything wet. Most

American PPV fans do not have this capability. A risk in using a PPV fan is the possibility of exposing smoldering debris to additional air. Caution should be used during the initial start-up cycle and firefighters should remain vigilant for signs of fire developing from the added air.

Structural Inspection

When all active fire has been knocked down, the first priority is to inspect the soundness of the structure and its support system. Beginning with an exterior scan, firefighters should reassess structural stability, fire damage, and signs of impending dangers. Working their way inside, firefighters should look for compromised support members, sagging floors, damaged ceilings, bowed walls, or any other signs that the structure is under stress. This process should be begin with the exterior during all fire operations and continued once overhaul has begun.

This process can be enhanced by using a TIC to read the building. While conducting the walk around, firefighters should be outside the collapse zone if possible. Beginning with roof stability, firefighters should inspect any structural damage caused by the fire, the amount of clutter stored in the overhead spaces, and pockets of soaked materials that are primarily supported by only one type of support. An example of this would be a large stack of debris that doesn't span two roof joists and is stacked high, exerting weight on just one joist. Without the second joist to distribute the load, the joist is in danger of failing, especially if damaged by fire.

If the building has a light weight frame, firefighters should closely monitor gusset plates and any support members made of engineered wood, such as an engineered I-Joist. These structural components make the building stronger in no-fire situations but can be deadly to firefighters. If firefighters find either of these two dangers, a closer inspection is needed.

Once the outside has been assessed, firefighters should work room to room in the same outside-in approach. Each room should be inspected at load bearing junctions for damage and each area should be opened up to better inspect the support members. Looking for signs of fire damage such as deep char or finding evidence of clean boards (boards that have separated from their original connections) are key factors in estimating stability. Firefighters may need to climb on the stacks of debris to complete this task and should move cautiously when doing so. A charged hose line needs to be close by in case an unexpected fire is found.

If at any point the crews discover that the structure is unsafe the OIC must be notified. Even if a victim's body is still located in the building, there should be minimal risk taken at this point of the operation due to the length of the operation and the fact that the crew is in recovery, not rescue mode. Removing firefighters from the building to outside the collapse zone should occur swiftly, and the OIC should begin to call in resources for building demolition.

Water Weight

Accounting for the amount of water added to a structure is a normal consideration for any structural fire. How much weight could be added to an already overloaded structure? Flowing 100, 200, or more gallons per minute multiplied by how long water flowed can give firefighters an idea of the amount of water weight that was added by doing the math. Consider 8.33 lb. per gallon x 300 GPM x 30 minutes This should give firefighters a perspective on the amount of weight the water has added.

A variable frequently seen in heavy content conditions is the inability of water to escape the structure. The belongings inside often absorb the water, adding to the danger of collapse. How much water can stacks of newspapers absorb, and how much do they weight once saturated? Many of the items collected are similar throughout the building and can absorb large amounts of water. Additionally, with the stacks of belongings blocking most all pathways, water cannot escape the structure, further adding to the weight accumulation. This added variable should be considered when estimating the load being placed on the structure. Firefighters may need to take action to reduce this risk by cutting small relief drains in walls and floors.

Debris removal

If the building is not at risk of collapse, firefighters can begin the overhaul process. Overhauling this amount of stuff is time consuming and very demanding on firefighters. Due to the dangers already mentioned in this chapter, all firefighters should remain on air and wear complete PPE. The process of assessing the need for complete debris removal versus leaving it in place should begin with the hottest location and progress to the coldest location in the building.

Calling for large dumpsters will aid in the extinguishment of the debris once removed from the building. Resources can come from local municipalities or by contacting the property owner's insurance company. Having this resource secured before the fire can lessen the response time. Placing the dumpsters close to the building, firefighters should use the pathways to begin the removal process. Using the window cut down process can aid in the removal process by shortening the space between stacks and the exterior.

If a dumpster is not available, firefighters should find empty spaces in the yard to spread the belongings out enough to ensure complete extinguishment. This process is painstakingly slow and can be aided with the use of buckets, wheelbarrows, or heavy machinery.

Working from hottest to coldest, firefighters can determine when and where the removal can end and the soak down can begin. Rooms showing only smoke damage may only require saturation with water, preferably enhanced water, to ensure complete extinguishment. If the stacks are still producing a large amount of steam or smoke they will need to be removed for further cooling. Re-kindle is a real concern when dealing with heavy content buildings, and every effort should be made to ensure complete extinguishment.

Incident Commanders should understand how this increased workload impacts firefighters during the overhaul phase of the fire. This workload is compounded by the need to wear SCBA and full PPE. Work periods should be shortened and rehab periods should be increased to compensate for this increased workload.

An example of these dangers occurred in Passaic, New Jersey on December 20, 2011. The Passaic Fire Department responded to a 2.5 story frame house with a heavy content environment. During the overhaul phase of the fire, Passaic sent 11 firefighters to the hospital with various injuries, from pulled backs to a broken arm. This fire demonstrated how dangerous overhaul can be due to an increased workload (11 firefighters injured in home of NJ hoarder, 2011).

Overhauling heavy content structures can swiftly turn into a technical rescue. Firefighters who suspect the building is compromised, even slightly, should retreat immediately.

CHAPTER 15:
EMERGENCY MEDICAL SERVICE (EMS) RESPONSE

Being tasked with dealing with a sick or injured patient inside a heavy content environment can expose responders to many different types of dangers. The lack of PPE use makes a medical call for service even more dangerous. Firefighters would never go into a fire without their PPE on, and neither should a responder entering a hoarding environment for an non-fire response.

Wearing the appropriate level of PPE will prevent the responder from being exposed to the different types of biohazards found inside the home. Using the applicable PPE for the conditions will ensure the responders' safety. Using one level higher than that of the conditions, or utilizing the maximum PPE is a wise choice to compensate for any unknown variables. Protecting the respiratory system should include the use of a N95 Respirator or an SCBA, as inhalation is one of the quickest routes for exposure. Using a SCBA is the highest level of protection available for responders. At minimum, a properly sized N95 respirator or APR should be used.

Natural ventilation should be a top priority for responders, even when wearing respiratory protection. Opening up doors, windows, and other pre-determined ventilation paths can help dissipate ammonia levels and allow fresh air in its place. Depending on the amount of clutter, this natural ventilation can be decreased. Consider using a positive pressure or negative pressure firefighting fan to help ventilate the area. Basic principles of using both should be applied.

To help reduce contact exposures, responders should wear an outer layer of protection. For non-fire EMS, this could include a Tyvek suit or a nylon jacket. When Tyvek is not an option, uniform pants should be tucked into duty boots, the jacket should be completely zipped, arms should be sealed with the wrists of rubber gloves, and hoods should be in place. This layer of protection will help reduce contact with any fecal matter or solid biohazards.

Responders tasked with managing patients inside a heavy content environment should consider performing a gross decontamination on scene and after patient removal. This process should follow local protocols and could range from a simple clothing removal to a complete wash down of the patient. The level of decontamination should be chosen based on conditions and the potential of contamination of EMS crews or hospital personnel.

If a gross decontamination cannot be completed in the field, utilizing a hospital's decontamination system is advised. Following local protocols, crews should notify the hospital as early as possible in order to activate needed resources.

EMS Size-up

For all non-fire based calls for service, responders should stay vigilant for cues and clues of heavy content. The likelihood of entering a non-fire hoarding situation is greater than in the past due to the increase in the volume of medical responses. Responders should scan for the signs of a cluttered environment and apply proper levels of PPE. Many EMS responders will need to add some factors to their normal scene size-up.

These factors include:
- Number of Animals
- Ventilation
- Expected Extrication Time
- Location of Patient
- Level of Hoarding (1-5)
- Status of the Building
- Exposure to the elements

These factors may be new additions to the size-up for a non-fire based EMS service. Early identification of conditions is essential to allow additional resources time to respond.

Animal control can be complex in cluttered conditions. Searching for animals that pose risks for responders is the first priority. In addition to the risk of injury from animals, the secondary risk is exposure to animals' waste products. Responders should be looking for animals and communicating with the occupant to establish their presence.

Multiple animal hoarding cases have found documented ammonia levels at 150 PPM. These findings illustrate the need for proper ventilation and respiratory protection. OSHA standards define an ammonia level of 50 PPM to be a hazardous environment and 300 PPM an IDLH environment

(Smith, J. 2014).

One of the first things responders should consider is the hasty removal of the occupant if necessary. This is the best option for both the occupant and responders when an occupant is found near an exit space where quick removal from the conditions is available. Retreating to the safety of the exterior, or the interior of an ambulance, will allow operations in a more controlled environment.

Lengthy extrications have also been documented in heavy content environments. Calling for the needed resources early in the response will improve the positive outcome for the patient. One variable responders should consider is additional EMS crews to relieve original responders. During a lengthy extrication, the initial crew can be facing an overwhelming workload, much like during a fire. Establishing the need for additional crew members and EMS rehabilitation time should be completed.

A need may arise for responders to enter a heavy content environment to locate an unaccounted-for occupant. It is common for responders to assist with welfare checks. Using the 380° size-up for non-fire calls and staying within the pathways is recommended. Occasionally the search can become more complex if the occupant is underneath stacks of belongings. Responders attempting to locate occupants should look for hands, feet, and mounds of belongings that appear to be out of place. Incorporating a TIC can assist in the search.

A case study from the Worthington, Ohio Fire Department (WFD) is a great example of the challenge of searching for a victim during a well-being check. The WFD was outside clearing snow away from fire hydrants when they noticed a home with frost accumulated on the inside of the windows, cars covered in snow, mail stacked in the mailbox, and other signs of no one being at home. The WFD firefighters called for law enforcement and requested permission to make entry for search. After forcing the door, WFD firefighters found a heavy content environment at a level 3-4 throughout the structure.

Firefighters found no interior heat, frosted windows, no running water, and no occupants. Upon deeper investigation, neighbors advised that the occupant would be inside the home as she had no other family and was rarely seen. Hours passed as the WFD searched throughout the home to locate the occupant. One firefighter suggested using the TIC and found the victim by locating a hand exposed from under a toppled stack of belongings. She was found under the stacks just inside the front door.

Unknown to the firefighters, she was underneath them the entire time, but due to the stacks of belongings they were unable to find her. A challenge when using the TIC in this situation was that the occupant was the same temperature as the surroundings. If it were not for the outline of the hand, they may have continued to overlook her (Pennington, 2014).

Perhaps the most unfamiliar size-up to non-fire based EMS is assessing structural stability. Looking for cues and clues is the same as it is for firefighters. The outside-in approach can help in this assessment, and once inside EMS crews should make strong efforts to keep the belongings in place. Localized collapse of the interior belongings could cause injury.

To aid in the reduction of collapse risk, EMS crews should leave large bags outside the structure and enter with minimal equipment. Doing so will limit their profile and increase the success of keep stuff in the stacks. By staging their non-essential equipment outside the structure it will reduce the exposures to biohazards as well. Sending one responder in with a portable radio while the other stays outside can be an initial tactic in severe cases.

Committing one responder to the interior will reduce the chances of disruption of the stuff while allowing the exterior responder to aid or call for help if needed. If the interior responder needs help, the exterior responder would be available to assist and not be trapped in the same location.

Victim Removal

Once the occupant has been found and treatment to stabilize has been started, the removal assessment should begin. Depending on the amount of clutter found, alternative routes of removal may be required. If established pathways will support it, a stair chair could be a viable option. Utilizing the carry handles and using it with both responders facing forward offers a more stable platform and allows for good communication between carriers. This is often accomplished by having the responder at the head level turn and face forward as the foot responder also faces forward.

If debris in encountered that requires them to step over it, both can work in tandem to clear the obstacle. By facing forward, both can scan for entanglement hazards that could attach to an occupant's shoulders or hands.

If the occupant is unable to sit, alternative methods of removal that offer responders additional leverage may be indicated. Such devices as Sked Stretchers, Reeves Sleeves, or backboards are examples of available devices. Dealing with the pathways can be difficult as these devices are long and stiff. Pushing a patient over stacks of debris could provide a semi-stable surface used for extrication. While not the ideal situation, it may offer a simple solution and a direct route. Responders should manage stacks in a controlled fashion, making all efforts to push the belongings away from their legs. This process can be physically demanding and place the occupant in a severely stressed situation if conscious. Supportive emotional talk should be continued to explain to the occupant the need to move belongings to aid in the extrication.

When moving and clearing a pathway, the most direct route of exit should be used. This may indicated occupant removal out of a window, side door, or require a wall breach to ensure the safety of all involved. Utilizing the appropriate resources is essential when dealing with the structural support of the building.

During complex removal situations, all responders must work in a coordinated fashion. A set command structure should be in place to coordinate exterior and interior operations. Additional resources should be called and staged to have a Rapid Intervention Crew ready in the case of emergency.

NOTES

Hoarder Homes

Sample Heavy Content SOG

I. SCOPE

This standard was promulgated to regulate the management of incidents involving structures where hoarding is an issue.

II. DEFINITIONS

- Heavy Content Fire: (politically correct term for) a fire in a structure that has excessive contents creating a large fire load and increasing the risk to firefighters conducting interior firefighting operations.

- Hoarding: is a pattern of behavior that is characterized by the excessive acquisition of and inability or unwillingness to discard large quantities of objects that cover the living areas of the home and cause significant distress or impairment. Usually compulsive.

III. SIGNS OF HOARDING

There are a number of evident signs of hoarding which can be identified during size-up. Each of these signs, in and of itself, does not mean there is hoarding but they should be taken as signs by the IC to investigate further as he is developing his attack plan. Signs include, but are not limited to:

    a. the presence of privacy fencing,

    b. cluttered exterior,

    c. blocked entrances,

    d. windows blocked by piles of material,

    e. excessive numbers of animals around the exterior,

    f. animal excrement around the exterior,

    g. unpleasant odors, or

    h. a lack of general maintenance around the building.

IV. **OPERATIONAL CONCERNS**

When operating at a fire in a structure with a heavy content level, the IC should be aware of the following concerns:

    a. excessive weight on the floor causing stress to the structure,

    b. increased fire due to increased fuel load,

    c. risk of electrical shock from exposed wiring,

    d. excessive animals and animal feces,

    e. risk of entrapment,

    f. narrow pathways through structure,

    g. blocked exits and windows,

    h. excessive workload for fire fighters,

i. residents may be over-protective of their belongings, and

j. residents may be introverted and reluctant to talk to responders.

- **RESPONSE TO HEAVY CONTENT FIRES**

    Upon identifying the fire building as heavy content occupancy, the following steps will be taken:

    a. announce to dispatch and to all incoming units that the fire is a "HEAVY CONTENT FIRE",

    b. Orient everyone to available exits and entrances

    c. consider starting in a defensive attack mode, particularly if it is known that all residents are out,

    d. appoint separate safety and accountability officers,

    e. call for additional resources,

    f. request police and additional EMS response.

- **OPERATIONAL PROCEDURES**

    Upon hearing the announcement that the incident is a "HEAVY CONTENT FIRE", all crews will adopt the following procedures:

a. if there is any indication that residents are still inside and they are deemed to be salvageable lives, all crews will follow these procedures:

   i. search and rescue crews will use a tag line attached outside of the structure,

   ii. interior attack crews will use a tag line in addition to their hose line,

   iii. water supply from a hydrant will be obtained prior to entry,

   iv. ventilation will be a coordinated closely with the entry crews, and

   v. a designated accountability officer will be assigned to control all entry to the structure.

b. If there is positive evidence that all residents are out of the structure, a defensive attack will be considered and adopted if there are any concerns for the safety of the firefighters operating at the scene.

- **<u>SAFETY PRECAUTIONS</u>**

   a. Be aware that a left or right hand search may not be possible due to materials stacked to the ceilings with only narrow passageways available for movement in the structure.

b. Be aware of possible collapse of materials into the narrow passageways.

c. In multi-family structures, be aware of fire extension through in-accessible walls.

d. Appoint a dedicated accountability officer to manage all interior crews.

e. Animals may be feral and could attack with little or no warning.

f. Be aware of contamination of gear and clothing and wash everything with an insecticidal soap after the incident.

g. Standard fire orders:

1. Be alert, keep calm, think clearly, and act decisively.

2. Maintain good communications at all times.

3. Give clear instructions and be sure they are understood.

4. Maintain control of your personnel at all times.

5. Fight the fire aggressively, but provide for safety first.

REFERENCES

11 firefighters injured in home of NJ hoarder. (2011, December 20). http://www.nbcnews.com/id/45738988/ns/us_news-life/t/firefighters-injured-home-nj-hoarder/#.VbfZSRNViko

American Psychiatric Association DSM-5 Development, (2013). http://www.dsm5.orgDocuments/Obsessive Compulsive Disorders Fact Sheet.pdf

Bratiotis, C., Schmalisch, C., & Steketee, G. (2011). Hoarding and Its Effects - The Hoarding Handbook: A Guide for Human Service Professionals. Oxford: Oxford University Press, USA.

COH Home Page. (2014, March 1). http://childrenofhoarders.com/

Dunn, V. (1992). Safety and Survival on the Fireground. Saddle Brook, N.J.: Fire Engineering

Books & Videos.

Frost, R., & Steketee, G. (2010): Stuff: Compulsive Hoarding and the Meaning of Things. Boston: Houghton Mifflin Harcourt.

Hanta Virus. (2014, February 20): http://www.cdc.gov/hantavirus/

Lucini, G., Monk, I., & Szlatenyi, C. (2009). An Analysis of Fire Incidents Involving Hoarding Households. http://web.cs.wpi.edu/~rek/Projects/MFB_D09.pdf

McCormack, J., & Pressler, B. (1998). Firefighter survival. Indianapolis, IN: Fire Department Training Network.

(NFPA 18, 2010, p. 18-6)

Oke, S. (2015, May 1). Kill the Flashover Project 2015. http://killtheflashover.com/kill-the-flashover-project-2015.html

Pennington, R. (2015, March 15). Hoarder Fire Case Study Elyria Ohio. http://chamberofhoarders.com/blog/entry/hoarder-fire-case-study-elyria-ohio

Prince, T. (2003). The NSGCD Clutter Hoarding Scale. National Study Group on Chronic Disorganization, (016). https://challengingdisorganization.org/content/clutte

r-8211-hoarding-scale

Reick, M. (2012, December 1). Smoke BlockAID – A portable smoke blocker for firefighting. http://www.rauchverschluss.de/RSS_e.pdf

Sarah Horner, S. (2012, December 21). Shoreview woman found dead in burning, cluttered home.

Scarpa, S. (2014, February 13). Hoarder Firefighting - Member Testimonials. http://chamberofhoarders.com/about/testimonials

Smith, J. (2014, June 1). POTENTIAL HEALTH CONDITIONS FACING HOARDING RESIDENTS. http://www.ci.fitchburg.ma.us/BoardofHealth/Health-Landfill/PHDIG-ResidentPhysiciansHoardingFlyer.pdf

Starnes, A. (2015, May 1). Kill the Flashover Project 2011. http://killtheflashover.com/kill-the-flashover-project-2011.html

Starnes, J. (2015, May 1). Kill the Flashover Project 2015. http://killtheflashover.com/kill-the-flashover-project-2015.html

Taylor, J. (2007). Smoke burns! York, England: Taylor Made Solutions (York).

Tony, K. (2015, April 7). Newsletter. http://www.kentland33.com/news/fullstory/newsid/219012

Whelan, A. (2014, February 14). N. Phila. man dies

after reentering his burning home. http://articles.philly.com/2014-02-14/news/47308308_1_edwin-walker-front-door-fire-commissioner-lloyd-ayers

Writers, S. (2015, March 1). Man Rescued From Fire; Firefighter Burned, Hospitalized - New Haven Independent. http://www.newhavenindependent.org/index.php/archives/entry/firefighter_rescued_victim_hospitalized/

ABOUT THE AUTHOR

Ryan Pennington is a Firefighter/Paramedic for the Charleston Fire Department in Charleston West Virginia. He is currently assigned to Station 6 that houses Quint 456/medic 436. He has over 20 years of combined Fire, Rescue, and EMS experience. Ryan started with a local volunteer department and continued through EMS to spend five years as a Critical Care Paramedic. Ryan transferred to the career fire service in 2003 and has worked for the City of Charleston since 2007.

Ryan Pennington is the Leading Authority and expert in Heavy Content Response. (Also Known as Hoarder Response). He is a highly sought out instructor, speaker, author, blogger and podcast host.

Ryan has lectured and trained thousands of firefighters and fire departments from across the United States and internationally both at their departments and at large conferences like Firehouse Expo, FDIC, Firehouse World, and FDIC Atlantic (Canada). He has been published in FireRescue Magazine, Fire Engineering, Firefighting in Canada Magazine, Firehouse, among others and has been interviewed on the top firefighter training podcasts and radio shows in the country.

He is the founder of ChamberofHoarders.com which is the leading Heavy Content Response Online Training Academy for fire departments worldwide. This website has the best heavy content online training with Heavy Content Firefighting Academy, heavy content fire news, case studies, interviews, podcasts, and more fully dedicated to training firefighters on the risks and best practices of heavy content fires.

Ryan blogs and podcasts about the views of a street level firefighters at JumpseatTraining.com.

To Learn more about Heavy Content Firefighting

and options for training your fire department, go to ChamberofHoarders.com or Contact Ryan at jumpseatviews@icloud.com and on twitter at @jumpseatviews

Made in the USA
Middletown, DE
18 October 2015